mocktails, cordials, infusions, syrups,
and more

mocktails, cordials, infusions, syrups, and more

OVER 80 RECIPES PROVING ALCOHOL-FREE DRINKS DON'T HAVE TO BE BORING AND BLAND

DOG 'n' BONE

Published in 2016 by Dog 'n' Bone Books
An imprint of Ryland Peters & Small Ltd

20–21 Jockey's Fields
London WC1R 4BW

341 E 116th St
New York, NY 10029

www.rylandpeters.com

10 9 8 7 6 5 4 3 2 1

Text © Maxine Clark, Lyndel Costain & Nicola Grimes, Tonia George, Beshlie Grimes, Carol Hilker, Lottie Muir, Fifi O'Neill, Elsa Petersen-Schepelern, Louise Pickford, Ben Reed, 2016
Design and photography © Dog 'n' Bone Books 2016

A CIP catalog record for this book is available from the Library of Congress and the British Library.

ISBN: 978 1 909313 91 0

Printed in China

Editor: Pete Jorgensen
Designer: Eoghan O'Brien
Photographers: Martin Brigdale 32; Peter Cassidy 64; Georgia Glynn-Smith 23; Jonathan Gregson 47; Gavin Kingcome 1R, 11, 66, 68-71, 74-76, 78-89, 91-100, 105, 110-119; Sandra Lane 73; Kim Lightbody 3, 8, 12, 60, 101-104, 122; William Lingwood 1L, 1M, 18, 22, 24, 26-27, 29, 33, 36-37, 39-40, 42-45, 50, 54-59, 62-63, 123; Mark Lohman 61, 126-127; James Merrell 46, 124-125; Noel Murphy 4, 48; Gloria Nicol 72; Steve Painter 7, 17, 65; William Reavell 21, 25; Lucinda Symons 10, 90; Debbie Treloar 30-31, 106, 108, 120; Ian Wallace 20, 33, 38, 40; Andrew Wood 2, 52

Contents

Introduction

"Do you have anything without alcohol?"

For such a simple question it's amazing to see the worried looks on people's faces as they struggle to think beyond offerings of fizzy drinks or an orange juice. Or the look of bemusement as they attempt to comprehend a night in a bar without booze. Luckily things are changing for the better, and not only are there more options available to non-drinkers, but also the questioning attitude toward people who choose a teetotal lifestyle is finally improving.

The reasons for staying away from the strong stuff are many—whether it's dedication to a healthier lifestyle or simply being the designated driver for the evening—but it never seemed right that by choosing to abstain from alcohol, drinkers had to sacrifice on taste. To cater for this ever-growing market, the following pages contain over 75 recipes packed with new and exciting flavor combinations, such as lemon and lavender, raspberry and rose, or apple and fennel. There are also drinks for all occasions, whether that's punches for parties and celebrations, mocktails to relax with at home, cordials and syrups that can be kept in the store cupboard throughout the year, delicious lemonades that are ideal for sunny days.

Many of the drinks featured also put an emphasis on using fresh produce that can be grown in the garden or easily found during a country walk. Ingredients such as elderflowers, mint, blackberries, and rhubarb can quickly be put to use in the Autumn Harvest syrup on page 92 or the Nojito mocktail on page 27.

It's hoped that by trying a few of these fantastic drinks, teetotallers and abstainers will never have to feel like they're being overlooked in the flavor department again.

Chapter 1

The Basics

General techniques

Here are some good tips for finding fruit, sterilizing, and storing your produce.

Sources of fruits

You can find fruit and herbs for drinks in many places, from your own garden to the supermarket.

Garden Planting and harvesting your own fruit and preserving its flavor in syrups and cordials is very satisfying and you will be able to grow lots of different varieties no matter where you live. If you don't have a garden, see if a friendly neighbor or relative can offer you some; many people find themselves with a glut of a fruit they are happy to share. You can then offer them a bottle of the delicious end product in return.

Countryside Plenty of fruit is to be had free from the countryside in late summer and early fall, such as elderberries, blackberries, and raspberries. A warning: avoid picking fruit alongside a busy road, where exhaust fumes will damage it, or at a low level where dogs might target it.

Farmers' markets These are a fabulous source of locally grown ingredients. If you have difficulty finding a particular fruit or herb that you need, always ask; producers can source most things.

"Pick Your Own" PYO farms are a fun day out, but the main attraction is the relative cheapness and quality of the fruit. Maybe not all the fruit will be uniform and beautiful, but it will most definitely have the fullest flavor.

Supermarkets Many people depend on supermarkets for citrus fruits and other hot-climate produce. There is no harm in this, but some fruits can be bland compared to locally grown produce. On the other hand, most supermarket fruit is fairly inexpensive so useful for making large batches.

Sterilizing

The job of sterilizing your equipment is the most important one when making syrups, cordials, and lemonades, and one cannot place enough importance on this part of the process.

Sterilizing bottles The sterilizing powder used in wine making can also be used for bottles you are using for syrups, cordials, and lemonades. Just mix the solution with water in a large bucket, using the proportions specified by the manufacturer, and use a pitcher (jug) and funnel to fill each bottle completely to the top. Pour away the solution after the required time and rinse as usual.

Alternatively, if using preserving jars, you can sterilize these in the oven, shortly before you need them. Wash them in hot, soapy water, then rinse in clean hot water and leave on a dish towel to air-dry. Lay the jars on their sides on the top shelf of the oven. Heat the oven to 225°F (110°C, gas mark ¼) for 20–30 minutes.

Straining

Some drinks must be strained to remove material from the liquid. For this you will need a sieve or fabric and a suitable container to collect the liquid.

Muslin A large square of fine muslin or cheesecloth is great for straining, as it can be folded for a fine strain or just left as a single thickness piece for a quick strain. You can use this by itself, tied up around the edges and suspended over a bowl, or use it to line a sieve.

Jelly bag This is a shaped bag, with three or four loops to hang it by, and sometimes comes with a framework of legs, for suspending it over a bowl while the juice drains out. The fabric is a little thicker than muslin and so can give a finer strain. Also, the bag can be washed many times. The only disadvantage is that these bags can be rather expensive.

Sieve A sieve, or strainer, is essential, as it can be used either by itself, for an initial strain, or lined with muslin to produce a clearer end product.

Storing

Various kinds of storage space are suitable for different drinks and production stages.

Cool, dark place This can be any place that is away from the fluctuations of your heating system and, of course, relatively cool. An old-fashioned pantry or corner of your basement or garage is ideal. The darkness also ensures that you are able to maintain a good color in your finished syrups.

Refrigerator The fridge is a good place to store your syrups and lemonades once they are opened.

Freezing

Both syrups and lemonades can be frozen. Try freezing them in ice cube trays; the cubes are the perfect size for an individual serving.

Diluted syrups and lemonades make wonderful ice pops. Freeze the liquid in molds or little plastic party cups, placing the sticks in the middle when semifrozen and then freezing them until solid.

Making Syrups, Cordials, and Lemonades

There's nothing more satisfying than drinking a cool glass of something you've produced yourself. Here's what you'll need.

Equipment

The following is a list of the items you will need to make your drinks.

Blender Use one that has the option of varying speeds and a reasonable-sized jar, so that you don't have to do many different batches.

Clear glass, large, sealable jars These are called "mason jars" in the U.S. and Kilner jars in Britain.

Coffee filters These do the same job as muslin or cheesecloth for straining very fine particles from an infusion, leaving a clear, sediment-free liquid.

Funnel Use one thin enough to fit inside a bottle.

Glass bottles These can be of the standard plain type that you can buy from wine makers' suppliers or pretty bottles that you have saved from other drinks, etc., but beware of any damage or fragility.

Heavy-bottomed, nonreactive saucepans
When using acidic ingredients, such as citrus juice, fruit, strongly colored vegetables, and brown sugar, use stainless steel, enamel, or lined copper; do not use aluminum, tin, or unlined copper because the lining of your pan will stain and might pit and peel off.

Ice cube trays Useful for freezing small batches of a syrup, so that you can use a little at a time. Use white trays, they are easy to check for cleanliness

Jelly bag This purpose-made, fine-mesh bag is used for straining the juice from cooked fruit.

Muslin/cheesecloth For getting a liquid as clear and particle-free as possible. Fold 3-ft (1-m) squares of muslin or cheesecloth into at least two or three layers thick and place inside a seive. Ensure they are clean prior to use—they are washable and can be used repeatedly.

Sieve This can be made of nylon or metal and should be at least 7 inches (18cm) in diameter; 8 inches (20cm) is better.

Choosing fruits, herbs, and flowers

When buying fruit, you'll naturally select healthy specimens, and if you've picked your own, you'll need to give it the same critical eye. Look out for any fruits that are rotten or unappetizing, and discard them. You need to use your judgment to ascertain whether the fruit or herb that you have picked is good enough to go into your chosen recipe. When using elderflowers, avoid brown ones; instead, look for lovely creamy white, open flowers; pick shiny, plump rose hips, as opposed to the ones that are starting to dry out. As a general rule, pick more fruits and herbs than you'll need for the recipe, to make sure of having enough usable ones.

In recipes containing lemon or orange zest, use unwaxed fruits, as it stands to reason that if you are zesting them you will not want to add wax as well. When picking flowers such as the elderflower or rose petals, wait to harvest these at the end of a warm day when their perfume is at its strongest.

Washing produce

Any fresh ingredients you buy or pick will need washing before use. When washing soft fruit, such as berries, take extra care not to squash the fruit, as you would lose the precious juice needed for your chosen recipe. Berries can be placed in a bowl of water and then gently scooped up with a sieve, allowing the water to drain out. Scrub fruit that has a rind, such as oranges and lemons, with warm water, as these may have been sitting on a supermarket shelf for some time.

Herbs can be rinsed under cold running water to remove any insects. The most difficult ingredient in this respect is elderflowers. Once picked, the stems can be gently shaken to remove any large insects; however, you will find that the elderflower will retain quite a few smaller ones. Place the elderflower in a bowl and leave it outside for an hour or so to allow most of the remaining insects to crawl away. You will not be able to eliminate all of the insects at this stage, but when you strain the liquid through fabric, any remaining insects will be removed.

Sterilizing tablets, powder, or fluid This is optional but makes sterilizing a large number of jars in a tub or sink that much easier.

Plastic bottles Any small water bottles can be used for freezing larger amounts of syrups; fill only two-thirds of the bottle—otherwise it will explode in the freezer!

Troubleshooting

Mold forming on top of syrups

This will occur if equipment and bottles have not been properly sterilized. Your only option really is to throw the syrup away; for even if you were to strain out the mold, the syrup would still have a nasty, almost alcoholic taste.

Making Mocktails

Producing delicious mocktails is addictive and once you get hooked the following advice will take your drink making to the next level.

Bar Tools

While it is perfectly possible to improvise with ordinary kitchenware, there are a few pieces of inexpensive equipment that make mocktail making more of a spectacle, easy, and fun.

Barspoon This is great for stirring, mixing, scooping, muddling, and layering.

Blender or juicer A good-quality blender and/or juicer is great for fruits like pineapple that are hard to juice by hand.

Citrus press A hand-held citrus press will make light work of lemon, lime, and small orange juicing.

Cocktail shaker There are two main types of shaker. The Cobbler shaker is made up of three parts: a pierced lid that acts as an strainer, a tall glass or metal beaker, and a cap that covers the strainer. The Boston shaker consists simply of a pint-sized mixing glass and a slightly larger metal tin that fits over it. It also requires a separate strainer. With either shaker, simply add your mocktail ingredients, fill two-thirds of the way up with ice, and cover with the cap or metal tin. The Boston shaker tin is a good indicator of when a drink is cold enough because it becomes frosty.

Cutting board and sharp knife These are essential for preparing your ingredients.

Fine grater A small Microplane grater will grate citrus zest and spices like nutmeg and chocolate with supreme ease and finesse.

Hawthorne strainer A Hawthorne strainer is designed to fit perfectly over the mouth of a Boston shaker to hold back the ice and large pieces of fruit and herbs as you pour your mocktail into the prepared glass.

Jigger or measurer Accuracy when pouring mocktails is vital, so invest in a precise tool to help you easily measure out the correct amount of liquid.

Muddler These tall, skinny tools are usually made of wood and used to release juices and oils in a glass. You can use the disc end of a barspoon or the end of a wooden spoon instead.

Punch bowl You can use a large pitcher (jug) or bowl but vintage ones make a great centerpiece.

Tea strainer Sometimes you will need to fine strain your mocktail and catch tiny particles like ice shards or fruit pulp. A tea strainer does this job very well.

Vegetable peeler Perfect for preparing garnishes.

Types of Ice

Ice and water are the important "weak" parts of your mocktail. Shaking or stirring your mocktail with ice doesn't just cool the drink—it can leave it consisting of up to 25% water, which is enough to balance out stronger ingredients. The different types of ice you can use serve different purposes, although, to be honest, you could make all the drinks in this book using standard ice cubes from a regular tray.

Cloudy vs. clear Cloudy ice is fine, but to make mocktails look extra special, clear ice is the thing. Boil distilled water and let it cool before repeating the process. Pour the cooled water into an ice cube tray and freeze in a closed container, so that the ice doesn't pick up other flavors lurking in the freezer.

Ice cubes Ice cubes are used for shaking, stirring, and serving. Larger ice cubes have a slower melting rate, so do a better job of chilling the drink.

Cracked ice Ice cubes that have been hit with the back of a barspoon in the palm of your hand, or wrapped in a dish towel and hammered. The idea is to increase the dilution rate for a drink by increasing the amount of surface area of ice touching the drink.

Crushed ice This comprises smaller sizes than cracked ice. It's the ice of choice for drinks that need to be weakened with water and it weighs down loose ingredients, such as mint, that you want to keep away from your mouth. To crush, wrap ice cubes in a dish towel and hammer it with a rolling pin.

Types of Glassware

Champagne flute Long, narrow-stemmed glass used to serve sparkling wine.

Collins/highball This is the glass of choice for a long drink with a mixer served over ice. Typically, a Collins glass is slightly taller and narrower than a highball, holding 10–14oz (300–420ml), whereas a highball is usually 8–10oz (240–300ml).

Coupe Attractive, bowl-shaped champagne glass that is popular for serving stronger mocktails.

Julep cup A metal cup made of pewter, silver, or copper that becomes wonderfully frosted as it chills.

Martini Also known as a cocktail glass, this is the classic, cone-shaped glass with a stem, holding 3–12oz (90–360ml).

Old Fashioned/Rocks Short and wide, heavy-bottomed glass, holding 4–8oz (120–240ml). It is sometimes called a Rocks glass because it is used for serving drinks over ice, or "on the rocks."

Punch cup Small and rounded with a handle, holding 6–8oz (180–240ml).

Shot 1-oz (30-ml) glass that can be used for sipping spirits or liqueurs neat or as a 1-oz (30-ml) measuring glass.

Wine Red wine is traditionally served in a large, bowl-shaped glass, allowing maximum access to oxygen, and therefore maximum flavor and aroma. White, rosé, or sweet dessert wine is served in a smaller, narrower glass that has been chilled.

Measuring

There is a need for accuracy when pouring mocktails if you want to achieve balance and consistency. Precise measurements are given in the recipes but they are not set in stone. If, for example, you prefer a sweeter taste, feel free to alter the quantities. When you come to devise your own recipes, you may wish to work in "parts," not cups, ounces, or milliliters. Simply assign a part to a measurement—for example, I part = Ioz (30ml)—then work out the ratios between the different ingredients and take it from there.

Mixing Techniques

It is easy to work out when to shake, stir, or roll. The end result should be a drink that's properly diluted (with ice and water), chilled, and evenly mixed.

Dry shaking This is what you do when there are egg whites in a mocktail. It involves shaking the egg white hard without ice for 30 seconds to allow the proteins in the egg white to coagulate and create a foam—they do this more readily when warm, hence the reason for not using ice.

Muddling You can use a proper wooden muddler, the disc end of a barspoon, or the end of a wooden spoon to lightly crush fruit or berries in a glass or shaker. The idea is to release the juices. For herbs, it is preferable to "spank" them in the palm of your hands to release the essential oils rather than muddling, which can bruise them and introduce some unwanted bitterness to the drink.

Rolling This involves chilling a mocktail with minimum dilution and frothing. Simply pour the mix into a mixing glass or shaker and then immediately "roll," or transfer, the whole mix, including the ice, into another empty mixing glass or shaker. Repeat back and forth between the mixing glasses until your drink is cold.

Shaking Mocktails that include fruit juice, citrus, dairy products, or syrups need to be shaken. Shaking produces a colder drink than stirring and allows for a bit more dilution of water. Put your mocktail ingredients into your shaker, then fill it two-thirds of the way up with ice cubes. Cover and shake hard for 20 seconds.

Stirring mocktails This stops the drink getting cloudy or frothy by introducing less air, and creates a more viscous texture. To stir a mocktail, pour the ingredients into a regular mixing glass or the metal half of a Boston shaker and fill two-thirds of the way up with ice cubes. Use a long-handled barspoon or the handle of a wooden spoon to stir the ingredients for about 20 seconds or until a light frosting appears on the outside of the glass.

The Pantry

The better quality the ingredients in your pantry, the better the mocktail.

Sugars You will see throughout the book that many drinks recipes require sugar or a sugar alternative. Superfine (caster) sugar is best for making most syrups. Raw, brown sugar is good for nojitos.

Salts A pinch of salt can counteract bitterness, and small grains of table salt are perfect for that. Salt rims can be a good way to enhance the flavor of a drink with a savory component, as well as looking and feeling attractive. Try to find good-quality kosher or sea salt for rims.

Milk and cream Sometimes you will want a mild, smooth element in a mocktail and a luxurious, creamy, and frothy texture. Very thick milk or, better still, heavy (double) cream with a high-fat content offer an extra dimension of texture and viscous mouthfeel.

Vinegar You can provide a wonderful umami, savory taste with the right balance of acidic and sweet using aged balsamic vinegar (see Strawberry Balsamic Shrub on page 35).

Spices There is a danger of storing so many herbs and spices that they go past their shelf life without being used. However, a few well-sealed spices, such as cinnamon, nutmeg, star anise, and whole cloves, can never go amiss, particularly in the fall and winter when you are out of many fresh herbs and want warming infusions and garnishes. Ginger is a great fresh spice to have to hand.

Herbs Dried herbs provide a stronger flavor than fresh; when making infusions, you need a third of the amount. Dried herbs are handy if you want to use them out of season or you need a herb that doesn't grow near you. Herb flowers have their most intense oil concentration and flavor just after the flower buds appear but before they open.

Soda water and mixers Some mocktails and lemonades, particularly long drinks served in a Collins glass, require carbonated mixers—soda water is the most common. Essentially, it is water mixed with sodium bicarbonate (carbon dioxide). The difference with sparkling mineral water is that it contains naturally occurring sodium bicarbonate but also a lot of other minerals that can

affect the taste of mocktails—hence soda water or seltzer being the preferred mixer. Don't get too worked up about it; the main concern is to use the contents of small bottles in one go, so the water doesn't go flat.

Citrus The essential acid component in many syrups, cordials, lemonades, and mocktails, to balance the sweet, derives from citrus. Organic, unwaxed lemons, limes, grapefruit, and oranges are all wonderful additions to your mocktails. Lemons provide a distinct lemon color, have a very clean, crisp flavor, and are less acidic than limes, with a pH of 2.2–2.5. Their white pith is extremely bitter. Limes, on the other hand, have a pH of 1.8–2, a green-colored juice, almost no pith, and a herbal complexity to the flavor. If you are lucky enough to find bergamots, yuzu, or other exotic citrus, use them as inspiration for some divine seasonal drinks.

Chapter 2

Mocktails

Orange Sunset

This vibrant and deliciously tangy juice is reminiscent of the classic Tequila Sunrise cocktail, with the beautiful colors of the orange and pomegranate evoking the early evening sun.

6 oranges
2 pomegranates

1. Peel the oranges, chop the flesh, and press through an electric juicer into a pitcher (jug). Halve the pomegranates and, using a lemon squeezer, squeeze out the juice into a separate pitcher (jug).

2. Pour the orange juice into two ice-filled glasses or tumblers, then pour in the pomegranate juice in a thin stream. Serve immediately.

Serves 2

Peach & Orange Nectar

You can select nectarines or peaches for this recipe, both of which add richness to the juice as well as providing a delicious additional blast of fruitiness to complement the orange.

5 ripe peaches or nectarines, halved, stoned, and quartered

3 oranges, halved horizontally

ice cubes, to serve (optional)

1. Put the peaches or nectarines through a juicer.

2. Use a citrus press or hand-held juicer to squeeze the juice from the oranges. Stir together the peach or nectarine and orange juices, then pour into 2 glasses. Add ice, if liked.

Now try this

Peaches work brilliantly well with cream, so for something a little more decadent add a dash or two of cream—it makes a wonderful after-dinner mocktail.

Serves 2

Sea Freeze

This non-alcoholic refresher is a play on the classic cranberry, grapefruit, and vodka cocktail Sea Breeze, but with the cranberry juice frozen into ice cubes. It's fun and ideal for summer sipping.

1¼ cups (300ml) cranberry juice

1⅔ cups (400ml) fresh grapefruit juice

old-fashioned lemonade, to top up

lime wedges, to garnish

1. Pour the cranberry juice into a 12-hole ice cube tray and **freeze** for at least 4 hours.

2. Divide the cubes between two tall glasses and add the **fresh** grapefruit juice. Top up with lemonade and garnish with wedges of lime.

Serves 2

Watermelon Lime Slushie

This mocktail is a twist on the Sharbat—a fruity concoction popular in North Africa and India. Here, the Sharbat has been turned into a slush and the recipe points up the flavor with a little lime juice.

1 small, ripe watermelon, chilled

2-inch (5-cm) piece fresh ginger root, peeled and grated

superfine (caster) sugar, to taste

crushed ice

2 limes, cut into wedges

1. Cut the watermelon in half, then remove and discard the rind and seeds.

2. Put the watermelon flesh and ginger through a juicer and blend until smooth. Add water if the mixture is too thick and add sugar to taste. Serve in glasses half-filled with crushed ice and finish by squeezing in the juice from a lime wedge.

Now try this

To make a frappé or granita, add sugar to taste (the mixture should be very sweet), then freeze in small, shallow containers. Just before serving, crush into icy shards and serve as a granita at the end of a meal. Alternatively, crush into an icy slush and serve as a frappé drink.

Serves 4

Pussy Foot

Grenadine is a classic cocktail syrup made from pomegranate, the sweetness of which counterbalances the sharp grapefruit. Any variety of grapefruit will work well here, but the ruby ones are a little less bitter. Try using freshly squeezed pineapple juice instead of grapefruit for a slightly sweeter variation.

⅔ cup (150ml) fresh orange juice

⅔ cup (150ml) fresh grapefruit juice

2 dashes of fresh lemon juice

a dash of grenadine

1. Use a citrus press or hand-held juicer to squeeze juice from the oranges, grapefruits, and the lemon.

2. Add the citrus juices and the grenadine to a shaker filled with ice cubes. Shake hard for around 10 seconds and strain into a highball glass filled with ice.

Serves 1

Citrus Fizz

This refreshing cooler is inspired by the Snow Angel cocktail, which adds a scoop of lemon sorbet to gin and orange liqueur. It's perfect for a party and can be served as a pre-dessert palate cleanser or as an after-dinner tipple.

5 oranges, halved horizontally

1 red or pink grapefruit, halved horizontally

2 lemon quarters

2 large scoops of lemon sorbet

sparkling mineral water, chilled, to top up

1. Use a citrus press or hand-held juicer to squeeze the juice from the oranges and grapefruit. Pour the juice through a strainer into 2 tall glasses and add a squeeze of juice from a lemon quarter into each one.

2. Add a large scoop of lemon sorbet to each glass and top up with chilled sparkling mineral water. Serve with a long-handled spoon.

Serves 2

Virgin Mary

This variation of the Bloody Mary must be one of the original mocktails and despite ditching the vodka it certainly doesn't suffer in the taste department. The ingredients combine to produce wonderful flavors, but don't be afraid to tweak the recipe to your tastes—a little extra Tabasco or pepper can really spice things up.

1¼ cups (300ml) tomato juice

2 grinds of black pepper

2 dashes of Tabasco sauce

2 dashes of Worcestershire sauce

2 dashes of fresh lemon juice

1 barspoon horseradish sauce

a celery stick, to garnish (optional)

1. Add all the ingredients to a shaker filled with ice. Shake and strain into a highball glass filled with ice. Garnish with a celery stick.

2. The ingredients in this recipe can easily be upscaled if you want to make a bigger batch for a few friends. A fun idea is to leave out the spices and allow people to season their own Virgin Marys.

Serves 1

Nojito

There's nothing in the manual that says cocktails with no alcohol in them should be low-maintenance or one-dimensional. This take on a classic is proof that alcohol-free definitely doesn't mean boring and bland.

6 fresh mint sprigs, plus 1 to garnish

1 barspoon superfine (caster) sugar

2 lime wedges

soda water, to top up

a dash of sugar syrup (see page 56)

1. Muddle the mint, sugar, and lime in a highball glass filled with ice. Top with soda and muddle gently.

2 Add sugar syrup to taste, garnish with a sprig of mint, and serve.

Serves 1

No-booze Piña Colada

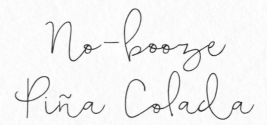

This non-alcoholic version of the kitsch Caribbean drink is delightfully indulgent and brilliant fun. Go wild with your garnishes—cocktail cherries, thick wedges of pineapple, plastic flamingo swizzle sticks, and cocktail umbrellas— the more colorful the better!

1 papaya

1 small pineapple

1 banana, peeled and thickly sliced

¾ cup (200ml) canned coconut milk

⅔ cup (150ml) thick yogurt

1. Cut the papaya in half, then scoop out the seeds with a spoon. Peel the papaya and cut into chunks. Cut the pineapple lengthways into quarters, then cut away the skin, remove the core, and cut the flesh into chunks.

2. Put the papaya, pineapple, and banana in a blender with the coconut milk and yogurt, then blitz until smooth and creamy— you may have to do this in 2 batches.

3. Go crazy with your garnishes!

Now try this

You can turn this into a lower-fat mocktail by using reduced fat coconut milk and bio yogurt, it will taste just as good as the full-fat version above.

Serves 1

Strawberry Mule

Perfect for an afternoon in the sun. Try substituting other fruits like mango, melon, or even rhubarb for the strawberries. They all pair brilliantly with fiery ginger beer.

1 teaspoon fresh ginger root, finely grated

3 fresh strawberries, plus 1 to garnish

ginger beer, to top up

1. Add the grated ginger and strawberry to a highball glass and muddle together.

2. Fill the glass with ice and top up with ginger beer. Give everything a gentle stir to combine the flavors and serve with two straws.

Serves 1

Thai Papaya Smoothie

The inspiration for this mocktail comes from Bangkok, where street vendors sell plastic bags filled with drinks—often luridly colored. Papaya is used widely in both sweet and savory dishes in Thailand, and here it's combined with another common ingredient, condensed milk, which is used to add sweetness and creaminess to the mixture.

10 ice cubes

1 papaya, peeled, halved, and deseeded

freshly squeezed juice of 1 lime

3 tbsp condensed milk

6 fresh mint leaves

1. Put the ice cubes in the blender and work to a snow.

2. Chop the papaya flesh and add to the blender. Add the lime juice, condensed milk, and mint leaves, blend again, then serve.

Now try this

If you don't have a tin of condensed milk lurking at the back of the cupboard, try using plain cream instead.

Serves 2

Chai Vanilla Milkshake

Chai is a fragrant spiced milky tea from India. This smooth grown-up take on a milkshake uses some of the same spices that feature in the tea, such as cardamom and cinnamon. Vanilla and a little sugar add sweetness.

4 cups (1 liter) full-fat milk

⅓ cup (75g) light muscovado sugar

2 tbsp black tea leaves

1 vanilla pod, split lengthways

¼ tsp ground cinnamon

8 cardamom pods

¼ tsp ground allspice

3 scoops vanilla ice cream

1. Put 3¼ cups (800ml) of the milk, the sugar, tea leaves, vanilla pod, cinnamon, cardamom, and allspice in a saucepan and bring to the boil.

2. Reduce the heat and simmer gently for 5 minutes, then turn off the heat, cover, and leave for 10 minutes. Strain into ice cube trays and freeze until solid.

3. When ready to serve, put the frozen chai cubes in a blender with the remaining milk and the ice cream and whizz until smooth. Serve immediately.

Serves 4

Cardamom Coffee Shake

The addition of dates and ground cardamom gives this iced coffee drink a definite Middle Eastern flavor—a real hint of the exotic. Cardamom improves digestion and provides a heady aroma known to act as an aphrodisiac. Dates and coffee create energy and enhance vitality and libido when combined, so perhaps this is the perfect drink for lovers!

4 Medjool dates, stoned

1¼ cups (300ml) organic milk

½ cup (125ml) cold espresso coffee

2 scoops vanilla ice cream

½–1 tsp ground cardamom, plus extra for sprinkling

1. Put the dates in a saucepan with half the milk and heat very gently until the milk just reaches boiling point.

2. Remove the pan from the heat and let cool completely. When cold, transfer the dates and milk to a blender and add the remaining milk, cold coffee, ice cream, and cardamom. Blend until smooth.

3. Pour into glasses and serve sprinkled with some extra ground cardamom.

Serves 2

Pineapple & Strawberry Crush

A summer mocktail that's the most glorious color and tastes like heaven! Strawberries in any guise please the palate and look wonderfully pretty. They're terrific with pineapple and sensational with rhubarb.

1 pineapple, peeled and cored

10–12 ripe strawberries, hulled

grated zest and freshly squeezed juice of 2 lemons

2 tablespoons confectioners' (icing) sugar, or to taste

freshly squeezed juice of 2 oranges

1. Put the pineapple, strawberries, lemon zest, and confectioners' (icing) sugar in a blender, add about ½ cup (125ml) iced water, and purée until smooth.

2. Add the orange and lemon juices and another ½ cup (125ml) iced water. Taste and add extra sugar if necessary (depending on the sweetness of the fruit).

3. Pour into a pitcher (jug) of ice and decorate with sliced strawberries and a twist of orange, lime, or lemon zest.

Serves 6–8

Strawberry Balsamic Shrub

Shrubs are cocktails made with vinegar as an ingredient—it sounds rather odd, but the mix of sugar, fresh fruit, and vinegar really works. Here, the balsamic acts like lemon juice, to point up other flavors, and its sweet, spicy undertones have an extraordinarily delicious effect. It also has special affinity with strawberries. Be warned: balsamic—the rich, slightly sweet, aged vinegar from Italy—should be used in moderation. Use it like a spice; your drink should be tangy, not unpalatably sour.

about 2 cups (250g) ripe strawberries, hulled

1 tbsp honey (optional)

6 ice cubes, plus extra to serve

balsamic vinegar, to serve

1. Reserve a few strawberries for decoration, then put the remainder in a blender with the honey, if using, and the ice cubes. Blend well, adding water if necessary to make the mixture easier to work.

2. Blend again, then serve in a tiny shot glass, over ice. Serve the balsamic separately, to add in drops.

Serves 2–4

Elderflower & Berry Cup

The berry ice cubes give this drink a pretty party feel. Make it in a large jug and let it sit for 10 minutes before serving—that way the ice cubes begin to melt, and the berry juices color the drink a delicate pink.

1¼ cups (150g) mixed berries, such as raspberries, strawberries (hulled) and blueberries

½ cup (125ml) elderflower cordial

sparkling mineral water, to top up

elderflowers, to garnish (optional)

1. Divide the berries between the ice cube tray holes and top up with still water. Freeze for 2 hours or until frozen.

2. Unmould the ice cubes into a large pitcher (jug) or 4 tall glasses and pour in the elderflower cordial. Top up with sparkling water, garnish with a few elderflowers, if using, and serve.

Serves 4

Berry Boost

Sweet strawberries, floral and fruity raspberries and blueberries, sharp cranberries—the mix of different flavors in this mocktail is as balanced as a circus tightrope walker. This is also a great cheat's mocktail—it uses frozen fruit so pick some berries up from the supermarket and you'll always have a go-to mocktail in the house.

1 cup (125g) frozen blueberries

1 cup (125g) frozen raspberries

1 cup (125g) frozen strawberries

1 cup (250ml) cranberry juice

1. Put all the ingredients in a blender and blend until smooth.

Now try this

If you can find fresh cranberries, add a handful to the blender and complete the recipe with 1 cup (250 ml) apple juice instead of the cranberry juice.

Serves 2–3

Bondi Rip

The name of this drink references Australia's most famous beach. After all, there are few better ways of watching the world go by than sipping fruit mocktails as the heat of the day fades and the sun worshippers head home for the night.

1 large mango, peeled, stoned, and diced

1 banana, peeled and sliced

1 cup (250ml) pineapple juice

¼ cup (50ml) raspberry syrup

6 ice cubes

2. Put the mango, banana, and pineapple juice in a blender. Add the ice cubes and whizz until smooth.

1. To serve, drizzle a little raspberry syrup down the sides of 2 tall glasses, pour in the blended fruit and ice mixture and stir well. Serve immediately.

Serves 2

A Cordial Relationship

The method below is for a quick blueberry cordial, but this is also the perfect recipe for trying out some of the mouth-watering syrups and cordials in chapter four. Recipes including the Black Currant Syrup (page 90), the Blackberry and Lime Syrup (page 80), or the Pear, Raspberry, & Elderflower Syrup (page 70) would be tasty alternatives to match with the apple juice.

2¼ cups (300g) blueberries

1½ cups (300g) sugar

sparkling apple juice, to top up

ice cubes, to serve

1. Place the blueberries and sugar in a large saucepan and heat gently until the blueberries soften and the sugar dissolves. Bring to the boil and simmer over a medium heat for 15 minutes, until syrupy.

2. Strain through a fine sieve or strainer and pour into a sterilized bottle (see page 11). Seal and leave to cool.

3. To serve, pour 2–3 tablespoons of cordial into tall glasses, add a few ice cubes, and top up with sparkling apple juice. The cordial will keep in the refrigerator for 4 weeks.

Now try this

Don't just experiment with different cordials, try topping up one of the lemonades in chapter five or an elderflower pressé.

Makes APPROXIMATELY 2 CUPS CORDIAL (500ML)

Raspberry & Apple Fizz

This is a truly refreshing drink for a hot summer's day, and with the addition of the sparkling water it makes a delightful mocktail that can be prepared in seconds.

2¼ cups (300g) frozen raspberries

1 cup (250ml) apple juice

12 ice cubes

sparkling mineral water, to top up

1. Put the raspberries, apple juice, and ice in a blender and blend until smooth.

2. Pour into 4 tall glasses and top up with sparkling mineral water.

Serves 4

Triple Goddess

Pomegranate, apple, elderflower, and lime combine to create a tangy effervescence in this mocktail. Try to find a pomegranate juice that errs on the slightly bitter side and the drink will balance perfectly, offset by the sweetness of the apple juice and elderflower.

⅔ cup (150ml) pomegranate juice

⅔ cup (150ml) cloudy apple juice

1½oz (40ml) freshly squeezed lime juice (about 1½ limes)

1oz (30ml) elderflower cordial

sparkling mineral water, to top up

an apple fan, to garnish

1. Add the fruit juices and elderflower cordial to an ice-filled highball glass and stir gently to mix.

2. Top up with the mineral water and serve garnished with an apple fan (see right).

Serves 2

Fenapple

Fresh fennel has a wonderful anise flavor that is surprisingly compatible with fruit. Mango, lemon, and black currant all love the hint of sweet liquorice in fennel, but the real dream union is with apple. Use a crisp, sweet red apple such as Red Delicious to give a wonderful pinkish tinge, and keep back a few of the fennel fronds to use as a garnish.

1 fennel bulb

2 apples, cored but not peeled

juice of ½ lemon (optional)

1. Trim the feathery green leaves from the fennel bulb (reserve a few sprigs), trim off the root end, then slice the bulb into long wedges and cut out and remove the cores from each wedge.

2. Cut the apples into wedges. Put the apples and fennel through a juicer.

3. Stir in the lemon juice to stop discoloration, then serve immediately, topped with the reserved fennel sprigs for extra scent.

Note

Fennel can be very difficult to juice—you need a strong machine. Alternatively, chop it and purée in a blender with apple juice, then strain. Always remember to remove the stem and stalk ends of apples and pears, as this is where any pesticides and residues collect.

Serves 1–2

Minty Ginger Granny Smith

Any apples will do for this drink, but unpeeled Granny Smiths produce the most beautiful green. Just a hint—apple juice adds natural sweetness to drinks, so you will not need any extra sugar here. Lime juice will stop the apple juice turning brown so quickly, but drink this concoction immediately—it won't hang around after you've taken the first sip.

4 Granny Smith apples, cored but not peeled, then cut into chunks

4–8 sprigs of fresh mint

a chunk of fresh ginger root, peeled and sliced (optional)

1 tbsp freshly squeezed lime juice (optional)

1. Push half the apples through a juicer, then the mint, ginger, and lime juice, if using.

2. Finally, push through the remaining apples and serve.

Serves 1

Jamaican Pineapple Ginger Brew

Ginger beer is a favorite drink in Jamaica. Put it together with fresh pineapple and you have an utterly delicious thirst-quencher—the taste of the Caribbean through a straw! Try it with other fruits, too, such as very ripe peaches, papayas, or apricots.

3 slices ripe fresh pineapple, chilled

about 1 cup (250ml) ginger beer, chilled

crushed ice

1. Put the pineapple in a blender, add about 2-3 tablespoons of the ginger beer, then the crushed ice. Blend well.

2. Pour the liquid into tall glasses or mugs and top up with the remaining ginger beer.

Serves 1–2

Pineapple & Mint Agua Fresca

Refreshing agua fresca is found all over Mexico. The name literally means "cold water" and it can be any fruit (or even another ingredient such as tamarind or rice and milk) blended with ice, sugar, and water. The idea is that it is cooling and rehydrating on a hot day. Serve it as a fruit frappé just with ice, or as a sparkling drink mixed with soda water.

½ cup (100g) granulated sugar

a pineapple (about 1lb 9oz/700g), peeled and cored

a small handful of fresh mint leaves, plus extra to serve

ice cubes, to serve

2½ cups (600ml) chilled soda water

1. Put the sugar andscant ½ cup (100ml) water in a saucepan and heat gently until the sugar has dissolved. Remove from the heat and leave to cool.

2. Cut the pineapple into rough chunks and place in a blender with the mint and the cooled syrup. Blend until smooth.

3. Divide the liquid between 4 tumblers with a scoop of ice in each one, or 8 tall glasses, and top up with ice and the soda water.

Serves 4–8

Kiwi Orchard

Apples and pears are classic bedfellows, grown as they are in orchards across the planet. Some of the finest examples come from New Zealand (you must try a Jazz apple if you haven't before, it's a taste sensation!), which is also one of the leading producers of kiwi fruit. This mocktail is a tribute to the New Zealand growers and it's an utterly delicious combination, with the ginger adding a surprisingly warm and lively note. If you can, try to use fruit that is only just ripe (or even a little underripe); if too ripe, the taste will be dull.

1 not-too-ripe pear
1 apple
2 not-too-ripe kiwi fruit

1-inch (2.5-cm) piece fresh ginger root, peeled

1. Peel and core the pear and apple and cut them into 6 wedges each. Peel and quarter the kiwi fruit.

2. Put the pear through the juicer first, followed by the ginger, kiwi fruit, and finally the apple. Stir well before serving, because it can separate. Drink as soon as possible!

Now try this

Put all the prepared fruits and ginger in a blender with ⅔ cup (150ml) plain yogurt. Blend until smooth, adding a squeeze of lemon juice or a little salt to taste

Serves 1

Chapter 3

Punches & Large Serves

English Summer Punch

Apples and cherries are a great flavor pairing and have been combined in desserts with great results over the years. The good news is, they work as well in a punch as they do in a cobbler or a crumble.

6 cups (1.5 liters) cloudy apple juice

½ cup (125ml) fresh lime juice (about 4 limes)

¾ cup (200ml) sparkling mineral water, to top up

10 fresh cherries, to garnish

ice cubes, to serve

cherry-infused syrup

1 cup (125g) cherries, pitted

2 cups (400g) superfine (caster) sugar

1. To make the cherry syrup, put the cherries in a blender and blitz for 1 minute. Put the blended cherries, sugar, and 1 cup (250ml) water in a saucepan set over low heat. Heat gently, stirring frequently, until the sugar is dissolved. Remove from the heat and leave to cool.

2. Add the cherry syrup, apple juice, lime juice, and mineral water to a large punch bowl filled with ice and stir gently to mix.

3. Serve in tall, ice-filled glasses, garnished with fresh cherries.

Serves 10

Tropical Punch

When making punches that involve whole fruits or fruit juices, always try and use the fresh fruit and juice or blend it, rather than using ingredients from cartons—the result will be far superior.

2 large ripe mangos, peeled, pitted, and roughly chopped

2 slices pineapple, peeled, cored, and roughly chopped

1⅔ cups (400ml) fresh pink grapefruit juice (about 4 grapefruits)

1oz (30ml) fresh lime juice

1-inch (2.5-cm) piece fresh ginger root, peeled

scant ¼ cup (50ml) sugar syrup (see page 56)

crushed ice

mineral water to thin (still or sparkling)

pineapple leaves, to garnish

ice cubes, to serve

1. Add all the ingredients to a blender with 1 scoop crushed ice and blitz until smooth.

2. Pour into ice-filled glasses and top up with mineral water to loosen the mixture, if required. Serve garnished with pineapple leaves.

Serves 2

Watermelon Cinnamon Punch

Although not the most common combination, watermelon and cinnamon do work well together. In fact, the delicate flavor of watermelon works well with many herbs and spices, including chili, mint, and even rosemary.

2 large watermelons, peeled and roughly chopped

1 cup (250ml) fresh lime juice (about 8 limes)

crushed ice

sparkling mineral water, to top up

block of ice, to serve

cinnamon-infused syrup

2 cups (400g) sugar

a pinch of ground cinnamon

1. To make the cinnamon syrup, put the sugar, cinnamon, and 1 cup (250ml) water in a saucepan set over low heat. Heat gently, stirring until the sugar has dissolved. Remove from the heat and leave to stand for at least 2 hours.

2. Put the watermelon in a blender with the lime juice, ¾ cup (200ml) of cinnamon syrup, and 1 scoop crushed ice. Blend until smooth. (You may have to blend the watermelon in batches if it won't all fit in the blender at once.)

3. Pour the watermelon mixture into a punch bowl and add a block of ice. Top up with sparkling mineral water, stir, and serve.

Serves 10

Snow in Florida

The Florida climate is perfect for growing amazing citrus fruits. But in that heat you need something to cool you down, and the sorbet here should keep the drink nicely chilled as it melts. This mocktail is quite sour; to make it sweeter just add a dash of sugar syrup (see below) or try using a different flavor sorbet.

4 cups (1 liter) fresh blood orange juice (about 17 oranges)

1 cup (250ml) fresh pink grapefruit juice (about 2½ grapefruits)

⅓ cup (100ml) fresh lemon juice (about 2½ lemons)

block of ice, to serve

8 scoops lemon sorbet

superfine (caster) sugar, to taste

soda water, to top up

1. Strain the freshly squeezed juices into a punch bowl with a small block of ice. Add the sorbet and a sprinkling of sugar and stir gently to mix.

2. Serve in punch cups or glasses topped up with soda water.

Note

To make sugar syrup simply mix together equal parts boiling water with superfine (caster) sugar and store in a sterilized jar or bottle (see page 11). The mix starts off cloudy but once it has cooled it becomes clear. It should keep in the refrigerator for at least a couple of weeks.

Serves 6

Tiki Breeze

Pineapple and mint are generally regarded as integral ingredients of the Tiki cocktail. Add fresh ginger, peach, and orange to this and not only have you got an authentic Tiki drink, but one with a subtle depth of taste that has all the goodness that a non-alcoholic cocktail can provide.

5 pineapples, peeled, cored, and roughly chopped

2 peaches, pitted but unpeeled

5 cups (1.3 liters) fresh orange juice (about 20 oranges)

a small handful of fresh mint leaves

3–4-in (8–10-cm piece fresh ginger root, peeled

crushed ice

ice cubes, to serve

1. Add all the ingredients to a blender with 1 scoop of crushed ice and blitz for 15 seconds. Pour into an ice-filled pitcher.

2. Serve in ice-filled highball glasses.

Serves 10

Cranberry & Fruit Punch

This colorful, fruity punch looks absolutely stunning with its rustic presentation—it's a true showstopper. It's based on the quintessential drink of the English summer—a Pimm's cup— and it's guaranteed to be a hit at any occasion where the sun is shining.

2 cups (250g) mixed fresh berries, such as strawberries, raspberries, and blueberries

1 orange, sliced

8 cups (2 liters) cranberry juice

1 small cucumber, peeled, seeded, and sliced

sparkling water or clear sparkling lemonade, to top up

ice cubes, to serve

1. Put the berries, orange slices, and cranberry juice in a large pitcher (jug) and chill for 1 hour.

2. When ready to serve, add the cucumber and some ice and top up with sparkling water. Pour into tall glasses or tumblers to serve.

Serves 12

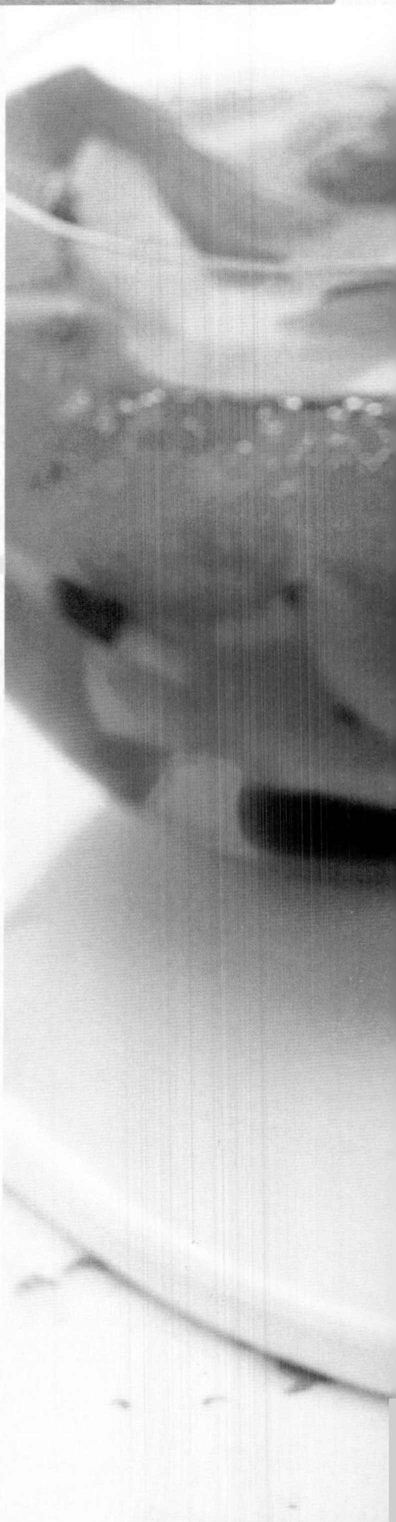

Lavender Honeysuckle

In a break from the traditional fruit ingredients that feature in many mocktail recipes, this drink looks to flavor itself by relying on some of the flowers found in many home gardens. Aromatic lavender and pretty honeysuckle are beguiling plants that also bring a unique, floral element to drinks. You can make this in quantity in advance and then top up glasses with soda water when required.

2 cups (640g) raw, runny honey

2 cups (500ml) warm water

2 heaped tbsp fresh edible-grade lavender buds or 4 tsp dried lavender blossoms

2 heads of acacia blossom (optional, if in season)

1 cup (250ml) freshly squeezed lemon juice

2 lemons, sliced into thin wheels

1 cup (20g) lemon balm (*Melissa officinalis*) or mint leaves

Splash of soda water

ice cubes, to serve

1. Combine the honey and water in a nonreactive pan and stir over a low heat until the honey liquefies and dissolves. Just before the liquid boils, add the lavender buds and acacia blossom heads (if you have them), remove the pan from the heat, and let steep for 20 minutes.

2. Strain the mixture using a fine-strainer or cheesecloth into the large pitcher (jug) (see page 11) to remove the lavender buds (and blossoms). Return the liquid to the cleaned pan, then add the lemon juice and the lemon wheels. Smack the lemon balm or mint leaves between your palms to release the essential oils. Add to the pan. Let stand for an hour.

3. If you wish, strain the mocktail punch again. Alternatively, remove the lemon balm or mint leaves and serve using a ladle. Fill 6 glasses with ice. Pour the punch two-thirds of the way up each glass. Top with a splash of soda water. Garnish with the sprigs of lavender and fresh sprigs of mint or lemon balm.

Serves 6

Spiced Pomegranate Apple Cider

There is nothing quite as satisfying as hot cider, especially on a nippy afternoon. Cloves spice up the natural sweetness of the honey, maple syrup, vanilla bean, and star anise. Delicious and comforting, this drink is equally loved by kids and adults. You can be sure they will ask for more so make extra batches. Just reheat them as needed.

16 cups (3.8 liters) pasteurized apple cider (juice)

2 cups (500ml) pomegranate juice

4 tbsp maple syrup

2 cinnamon sticks

6 whole cloves, plus extra for garnishing (optional)

½ vanilla bean (pod)

3 star anise

4 oranges, peeled, zest reserved

2 sliced oranges, for garnishing (optional)

1. In a large pan combine the cider, pomegranate juice, and maple syrup.

2. Add the cinnamon sticks, cloves, vanilla bean, star anise, and orange zest. Bring mixture to a boil; reduce heat. Cover and simmer for 15 minutes. Strain to remove all solids.

3. Serve warm, garnished with clove-studded orange slices if desired.

Now try this

You can either discard the four oranges that are needed for the zest, or juice them and add the juice to the apple cider and pomegranate juice.

Serves 16

Jasmine & Lychee Iced Tea

This is a delicately flavored iced tea, full of exotic character. If you are lucky enough to find fresh lychees you can use those and simply add a little honey for sweetness, otherwise canned lychees in a light syrup will work well too.

1 tbsp Jasmine tea leaves

4 cups (1 liter) just-boiled water

2 star anise, bashed lightly

14oz (400g) fresh lychees (or canned lychees in syrup), deseeded

honey, to taste (optional)

clear sparkling lemonade, to top up

lime wedges

sprigs of fresh mint

ice cubes, to serve

1. Put the tea leaves in a warmed teapot or heatproof pitcher (jug) and pour in the just-boiled water. Leave to infuse for 5 minutes, then strain the tea into a clean pitcher (jug). Add the star anise and let cool.

2. Half-fill 6 tall glasses with ice and add 3 lychees and a dash of honey if the fruit is fresh, or 2 tablespoons of the syrup if canned, to each one. Add a few lime wedges and mint sprigs to the glasses and top up with lemonade to serve.

Serves 6

PUNCHES & LARGE SERVES

Thai-ced Tea

There are so many different ways of making Thai tea, but there's a richness to this variation thanks to the addition of cardamom, cloves, and cinnamon. Serve cold over ice.

6 cups (1.45 liters) water

1 cup (60g) Thai tea leaves

4 cardamom pods, crushed

1 whole clove, crushed

¼ teaspoon cinnamon

1 cup (200g) granulated sugar

(US) 1 cup half and half or (UK) 120 ml double cream and 120 ml whole milk, mixed

crushed ice, to serve

1. In a medium saucepan, bring the water to the boil. Stir in the tea leaves and crushed cardamom pods, crushed clove, and cinnamon.

2. Cover and remove the mixture from heat and let steep for 5 minutes.

3. Pour the brewed tea through a fine wire-mesh sieve or strainer into a heatproof pitcher (jug), discarding the tea leaves. Add the sugar, and stir until it has dissolved; cool. Cover and chill for 2 hours.

4. Serve in glasses over crushed ice. Top with a couple of tablespoons of the half and half (or cream mixture) and it's ready to drink!

Now try this

Black tea leaves make a good substitution for Thai tea leaves in this recipe, but for a real treat see if you can get hold of some black vanilla tea, the additional flavor is irresistible.

Serves 6—8

Iced Louisiana Apricot Tea

Iced teas are a typical Louisiana-style refreshment. Served in tall, elegant glasses, iced tea is a drink that's well suited to the grand colonial homes prevalent in this part of the US. Fresh peaches or nectarines can be used instead of apricots, if preferred.

4 orange pekoe tea bags

2 sprigs of fresh rosemary, plus extra to garnish

4 cups (1 liter) just-boiled water

1¼ cups (300ml) apricot nectar

6 fresh apricots, halved, stoned, and sliced

sparkling mineral water, to top up

ice cubes, to serve

1. Put the tea bags and rosemary in a heatproof pitcher (jug) and pour in the just-boiled water. Leave to steep for 10 minutes, then remove and discard the tea bags. Let cool, chill for 1 hour, and then remove and discard the rosemary.

2. Stir in the apricot nectar, apricots, and ice cubes and pour into tall glasses. Top up each drink with sparkling mineral water and garnish with a sprig of rosemary to serve.

Serves 6

Chapter 4
Syrups & Cordials

Elderflower Syrup

One of the earliest harvests you can employ in making syrups, elderflower evokes the promise of a long, lazy summer about to begin.

20 heads of elderflower
(see page 13)

2 unwaxed lemons

10 cups (1.8kg) superfine
(caster) sugar

5 cups (1.2 liters) water

$\frac{3}{8}$ cup (75g) citric acid

1. Shake the elderflower heads to remove any lingering insects, remove the stems, and place in a large mixing bowl. Peel the zest from the lemons, then slice them. Add the zest and lemon slices to the bowl.

2. Put the sugar and water into a pan and bring to a boil, stirring until all the sugar has dissolved.

3. Pour the sugar syrup over the elderflower heads and lemon, add the citric acid, and give the contents a good stir.

4. Cover the mixture with a clean dish towel and let steep for 24 hours.

5. Strain the mixture through a sieve lined with fine muslin or cheesecloth (see page 11).

6. Pour the syrup into sterilized bottles (see page 11) and store in a cool, dark place. Use within 3 months. Alternatively, freeze in small plastic containers (see page 11).

Makes APPROXIMATELY 5 CUPS (1.2 LITERS)

Blueberry & Elderflower Syrup

Elderflower has a wonderful perfume, which beautifully complements the great flavor of blueberries. To take full advantage of its fleeting season, this recipe makes a large batch of syrup. A lovely way to enjoy this syrup is to pour a little in a blender, add some vanilla ice cream and some milk, and blitz briefly to combine. Garnish with a few blueberries and enjoy a scrumptious blueberry milkshake.

20 large heads of elderflower (see page 13)

2 unwaxed lemons

3 cups (400g) blueberries (fresh or frozen)

2½ cups (550g) superfine (caster) sugar

1 teaspoon citric acid

5 cups (1.2 liters) water

1. Remove the stems of the elderflowers as close to the heads as possible, then shake the flowers to remove any persistent insects. Place the flowers in a large mixing bowl. Cut the lemons into quarters.

2. Put the blueberries, sugar, lemon, citric acid, and water in a large pan. Bring to a boil then reduce the heat and let the mixture simmer for 15–20 minutes, squashing the berries with a potato masher or the back of a spoon.

3. Once all the berries are reduced to a pulp, pour the mixture into the bowl containing the elderflowers, making sure they are completely covered (use the back of a wooden spoon to push them in, if necessary). Cover the bowl with a clean dish towel and let steep overnight.

4. Strain the mixture through a fine sieve; if you want a really clear syrup, strain it again through a jelly bag (see page 11).

5. Pour the syrup into sterilized bottles (see page 11); use within 3 months. Alternatively, freeze in smaller containers (see page 11).

Makes APPROXIMATELY 10 CUPS (2.5 LITERS)

Pear, Raspberry, & Elderflower Syrup

This recipe, featuring the delicate perfume of elderflowers, is a must try. You'll need to make it when elder is in bloom, so will probably have to use out-of-season pears and raspberries from the supermarket. Frozen raspberries are fine, but make sure that the pears are really ripe before using them.

1¼lb (600g) pears

20 heads of elderflower (see page 13)

⅞ cup (200g) superfine (caster) sugar

2 lemons, juice only

1 lime, zest only

¾ teaspoon citric acid

3 cups (750ml) water

1¾ cups (200g) raspberries

1. Chop the pears into little chunks (no need to peel or core). Shake the elderflower heads really well to ensure that any insects are removed, then place them in a bowl and set aside.

2. Put the sugar, lemon juice, lime zest, citric acid, and water in a pan and bring to a boil, stirring until all the sugar is dissolved. Reduce the heat, add the pears and raspberries, and simmer for 15 minutes. Remove from the heat and allow to cool for 20 minutes.

3. Pour the pear and raspberry mixture over the elderflowers. Cover with a clean dish towel and leave overnight to steep.

4. Strain the mixture through a fine sieve (see page 11); repeat if necessary to make sure all the elderflowers are removed.

5. Pour the syrup into sterilized bottles (see page 11) and store in a cool, dark place and use within 3 months.

Makes APPROXIMATELY 3½ CUPS (800ML)

Elderberry & Clove Syrup

As well as having a rich, earthy fruitiness, this syrup, made from the most common of shrubs, *Sambucus nigra*, is best known as a winter tonic, boosting the immune system and helping to fight flu, either as a preventive medicine or as a symptomatic treatment.

25 heads of elderberries
at least 4 cups (1 liter) water

3¾ cups (750g) superfine
(caster) sugar
12 cloves

1. Strip the berries from the stems using your fingers or a fork. Rinse the berries, then add to a nonreactive pan. Pour in enough water to cover them (at least 4 cups/1 liter). Bring to a boil and let simmer on a low heat until the berries are softened (about 20 minutes).

2. Mash the berries gently to ensure all the juice has been released. Remove from the heat and strain the berries into a wide-mouthed measuring cup. You should have just over 4 cups (1 liter) of juice. Add the sugar and cloves. Return the liquid, sugar, and cloves to the cleaned pan and bring to a boil. Let simmer for a further 10 minutes. Remove from the heat and funnel into the sterilized bottle(s) (see page 11). Divide the cloves up equally between the bottles and seal.

3. Store in a cool, dark place, where the syrup will last for up to a year. Once opened, keep in the refrigerator for up to 2 months. You may wish to remove the cloves after a time if their flavor becomes too strong.

Makes APPROXIMATELY 4 CUPS (1 LITER)

Crab Apple Syrup

This beautiful, orangey-pink, floral-scented, autumnal syrup could not be further removed from the jaw-clenching sourness of a green or red uncooked crab apple. The recipe requires patience: the crab apple juice has to drip, drop by drop, through a very fine strainer or several layers of cheesecloth, otherwise it will turn cloudy. It's best to leave it overnight to resist the temptation of giving it a prod.

3¼lb (1.5kg) crab apples

3½ cups (700g) superfine (caster) sugar

juice of ½ lemon

1. Wash the crab apples and remove any stems, greenery, and blossom ends. Don't bother to core the apples but if they are golf-ball size or bigger, cut them in half. Place in a nonreactive pan and pour in just enough water to cover. Bring to a boil and let simmer until the apples are soft (about 25 minutes).

2. Strain the pulp carefully through a jelly bag or several layers of cheesecloth suspended above a large bowl or pan (see page 11). Let the pulp move through the filter very slowly.

3. Measure your final amount of juice, and for every 4 cups (1 liter), add 3½ cups (700g) sugar. Add the juice and sugar to the cleaned pan and bring to a boil. Then add the lemon juice and boil hard for about 10 minutes until you have a syrup consistency. Skim off any froth.

4. Carefully funnel the syrup into the sterilized bottle(s) (see page 11) and seal. Store in a cool, dark place. Once opened, consume within a month.

Makes APPROXIMATELY 4 CUPS (1 LITER)

Lemon & Lavender Syrup

The heady scent of lavender growing in the garden is intoxicating, but it can also be used indoors as an amazingly versatile cooking ingredient. Besides being useful for sweetening stewed fruit and other desserts, it complements many meat dishes, too; try it in a simple lamb casserole, for example. Be sure to use the common lavender, *Lavandula angustifolia*, rather than the more unusual species.

10–12 heads of lavender

3 unwaxed lemons, juice and zest

1¼ cups (300g) superfine (caster) sugar

6 cups (1.4 liters) water

1½ teaspoons citric acid

1. Rinse the lavender heads under cold running water and set aside.

2. Put the lemon juice in a large pan and add the sugar, water, and citric acid. Bring to a boil. Add the lavender and allow to simmer for another 10 minutes. Remove from the heat and let cool for 1 hour.

3. Strain the syrup through a piece of muslin (see page 11).

4. Pour the syrup into sterilized bottles (see page 11) and store in a cool, dark place. Use within 3 months.

Now try this

Embellish a drink made from this syrup and sparkling water with a slice of lemon and some ice cubes in which you have frozen some lavender heads. Or mix the cordial with some confectioners' (icing) sugar to make a simple icing for a cake.

Makes APPROXIMATELY 6 CUPS (1.4 LITERS)

Lemon & Thyme Syrup

Despite its unconventional ingredient—an herb normally associated with savory dishes—this syrup has won over many a skeptic. Try it yourself; you may be surprised how much you like it. For a piquant dessert, try adding some of this syrup to the filling for lemon meringue tartlets.

bunch of fresh thyme, or
4 teaspoons dried thyme

4½ cups (1 liter) lemon juice (about
16 lemons, preferably unwaxed)

zest from 4 of the lemons

2¼ cups (500g) superfine
(caster) sugar

2 cups (500ml) water

1 teaspoon citric acid

1. Rinse the thyme, if using fresh (see page 13).

2. Put the lemon juice and zest in a large pan, along with the sugar, thyme, water, and citric acid, and bring to a boil. Reduce heat and simmer for 20 minutes. Remove from the heat, cover with a saucepan lid or dish towel, and let cool for 2 hours.

3. Strain through a piece of muslin (see page 11).

4. Pour the syrup into sterilized bottles (see page 11). Store in a cool, dark place. Use within 3 months.

Makes APPROXIMATELY 6 CUPS (1.4 LITERS)

Honey & Lemon Syrup

We all know how soothing honey and lemon are when we have a cold, but they also make a surprisingly pleasant base for a cool drink. The taste will vary according to the kind of honey you select. Ordinary store-bought honey is fine, but you might like to try experimenting with lavender or lime honey, or source some honey from a local beekeeper.

1½ cups (500g) clear honey

1 large lemon, juice only

4 cups (1 liter) water

4 teaspoons tartaric acid

1. Heat the honey in the microwave at the 450w/low setting (remember to remove the lid first), for 1 minute only; the honey should not be any hotter than 160°F (70°C), as this would impair the flavor.

2. Pour the honey into a 1-quart (1-liter) pitcher (jug); add the lemon juice.

3. Boil the water, then allow it to cool until it is lukewarm. Add it, along with the tartaric acid, to the pitcher, filling it up to about 1 inch (3cm) from the top and stir well to blend thoroughly. If necessary, put the pitcher into the microwave for 1 minute to make sure the honey is dissolved.

4. Pour the contents into sterilized bottles (see page 11) and store in a cool, dark place. Use within 3 months. Freezing this syrup is not recommended as it would cause the honey to crystallize and could impair the flavor.

Makes APPROXIMATELY 4 CUPS (1 LITER)

Ginger Syrup

Ginger root has long been used in folk medicine and is a great soother of the stomach. But unlike many medicinal herbs and spices, ginger is delicious and makes a fantastic syrup. If you like your ginger drinks really fiery, use a bit more ginger than specified in the ingredients. With its lemon content this syrup pairs beautifully with fizzy lemonade and a slice of lemon. You might also pour a little over lemon sorbet and top with some crystallized ginger.

3 ounces (85g) ginger root, or more to taste

1¼ cups (300g) superfine (caster) sugar

1¾ cups (400ml) water

1¾ cups (400ml) lemon juice (about 9 or 10 lemons)

¾ teaspoon citric acid

1. Coarsely mash the ginger root using a mortar and pestle.

2. Put the ginger in a pan along with the sugar and water and bring to a boil. Reduce the heat and allow to simmer for 15 minutes.

3. Add the lemon juice and citric acid and bring the mixture back to a boil. Allow to cool for 1 hour.

4. Strain the mixture through a piece of fine muslin or cheesecloth (see page 11).

5. Pour the syrup into sterilized bottles and store in a cool, dark place; use within 3 months.

Makes APPROXIMATELY 2½ CUPS (600ML)

Gooseberry & Lemon Balm Syrup

If gooseberries are not readily available from local supermarkets, why not grow your own? (Check with a garden center to find a good cultivar for your area.) This underestimated fruit has many uses—in desserts and sauces for meat and fish. It also has health benefits, being packed with fiber and vitamins A and C.

1¾ cups (400g) gooseberries

8 sprigs fresh lemon balm (preferably young leaves)

1¼ cups (280g) superfine (caster) sugar

1 unwaxed lemon, juice and zest

1 teaspoon citric acid

4 cups (1 liter) water

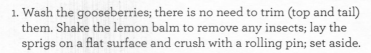

1. Wash the gooseberries; there is no need to trim (top and tail) them. Shake the lemon balm to remove any insects; lay the sprigs on a flat surface and crush with a rolling pin; set aside.

2. Put the gooseberries in a pan along with the sugar, lemon juice and zest, citric acid, and water. Bring to a boil, then reduce the heat and leave the mixture to simmer for 10 minutes, or until the gooseberries are soft. Mash with the back of a spoon. Remove from the heat and let cool for about 45 minutes.

3. Strain the mixture through a piece of fine muslin or cheesecloth (see page 11), pushing on the pulp to extract every last bit of flavor.

4. Pour the syrup into sterilized bottles (see page 11) and store in a cool, dark place. Use within 3 months. Alternatively, it can be frozen (see page 11).

Makes APPROXIMATELY 5 CUPS (1.2 LITERS)

Gooseberry & Elderflower Syrup

If you're lucky enough to live in a part of the world where fresh gooseberries are readily available, make the most of them by making this light, refreshing syrup. For a culinary twist, you could try adding some to a salad of mixed cantaloupe and honeydew melon (use a melon baller for a pretty effect) and prosciutto.

1¾ cups (400g) gooseberries

5 or 6 large heads of elderflower (see page 13)

1¼ cups (280g) superfine (caster) sugar

1 unwaxed lemon, juice and zest

4 cups (1 liter) water

1 teaspoon citric acid

1. Rinse the gooseberries under cold water. There is no need to trim (top and tail) them. Wash the elderflowers (see page 13) and put them in a large mixing bowl.

2. Put the gooseberries, sugar, lemon juice and zest, and water in a large pan and bring to a boil. Reduce the heat and simmer for 15 minutes. Make sure that all the gooseberries have softened to a pulp, mashing them with the back of the spoon, if necessary. Remove from the heat and let cool for 1 hour.

3. Pour the gooseberry mixture over the elderflowers. Cover with a clean dish towel and let steep overnight.

4. Strain the mixture through a sieve lined with fine muslin or cheesecloth (see page 11).

5. Pour the syrup into sterilized bottles (see page 11) and store in a cool, dark place. Use within 3 months.

Makes APPROXIMATELY 5 CUPS (1.2 LITERS)

Blackberry & Lime Syrup

Blackberries can be found in abundance from late summer into fall. Children especially love to pick blackberries, although most go into the mouth even before they can get to the kitchen. Try using this syrup on lime sorbet or chocolate ice cream.

12 cups (1.5kg) blackberries
1 lime
7 cups (1.6 liters) water

1¾ cups (400g) superfine (caster) sugar
1½ teaspoons citric acid

1. Pick over the blackberries, discarding any rotten ones. Rinse them under cold running water, being careful not to break their skins, as you need to retain as much juice as possible. Grate about 1 teaspoon of zest from the lime, then squeeze the lime to extract the juice.

2. Place the berries in a pan and cover them with the water. Bring them to a boil and allow to simmer until they burst, using a potato masher to facilitate this if necessary.

3. Strain the berry juice through a metal sieve into a clean saucepan (see page 11).

4. Add the sugar, lime juice and zest, and citric acid to the berry juice. Bring to a boil and stir until the sugar has dissolved. Let the syrup cool for at least 1 hour.

5. Pour the syrup into sterilized bottles (see page 11) and store in a cool, dark place, where it will keep for up to 3 months. Alternatively, place it in plastic containers (see page 11) and freeze it.

Makes APPROXIMATELY 6½ CUPS (1.5 LITERS)

Strawberry & Black Pepper Syrup

More than any other fruit, strawberries seem to conjure up the essence of summer. Black pepper might seem an unusual ingredient to add to strawberries, but it brings out the sweetness of the berries, intensifying their flavor.

4½ cups (500g) strawberries (5 cups if large)

4 cups (900g) superfine (caster) sugar

½ teaspoon freshly ground black pepper

1 unwaxed lemon

2 cups (500ml) water

1½ teaspoons citric acid

1. Mash the strawberries and sugar together in a bowl, using a potato masher. Sprinkle the black pepper over the mixture and gently stir in.

2. Cut the lemon into wedges and put them in a saucepan with the water. Bring to a boil and then simmer for 15 minutes.

3. Add the strawberry mixture and the citric acid to the lemon and water. Stir in and bring to a gentle simmer; let simmer for another 25 minutes. Remove from the heat. Cover with a clean dish towel and allow to cool for at least 2 hours.

4. Strain the cooled syrup through a fine sieve, pressing gently on the pulp in the sieve to squeeze out the last few drops of liquid (see page 11).

5. Pour the syrup into sterilized bottles (see page 11) and store in a cool, dark place. To serve, dilute to taste. Use within 3 months of making.

Makes APPROXIMATELY 5 CUPS (1.2 LITERS)

Now try this

This cordial is delicious on meringues or simply drizzled on plain yogurt.

Strawberry & Mint Syrup

Bought strawberries, in season, are fine; but if possible, grow your own. There is a special excitement to be had from lifting a leaf in a strawberry patch and finding a plump, warm fruit waiting to be picked. In this syrup the mellow flavor of strawberries is given extra zing with fresh mint. Try blending some of this syrup into some plain yogurt. Serve with a sprig of mint and some pistachio cookies on the side.

5 sprigs fresh mint

⅝ rounded cup (150g) superfine (caster) sugar

½ unwaxed lemon

3 cups (700ml) water

4½ cups (500g) strawberries (5 cups if large)

½ teaspoon citric acid

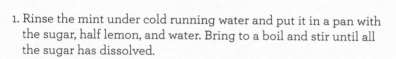

1. Rinse the mint under cold running water and put it in a pan with the sugar, half lemon, and water. Bring to a boil and stir until all the sugar has dissolved.

2. Reduce the heat and add the strawberries and citric acid. Simmer until all the strawberries are soft. Cover with a clean dish towel and let cool and steep overnight.

3. Strain the syrup through a sieve (see page 11).

4. Pour into sterilized bottles (see page 11) and store in a cool, dark place; use within 3 months. Alternatively, freeze in small portions (see page 11).

Makes APPROXIMATELY 3 CUPS (700ML)

Strawberry & Lavender Syrup

The versatility of lavender is quite amazing. It is used in perfume, to scent linens, as a room fragrance, and even in baking. Here, it gives a lovely aromatic note to a strawberry syrup. This recipe will give you a renewed appreciation of this little flower.

½ unwaxed lemon, juice and zest

⅝ cup, rounded (150g) superfine (caster) sugar

2 cups (500ml) water

4½ cups (500g) hulled strawberries (5 cups if large)

20 heads of lavender (see page 13)

½ teaspoon citric acid

1. Put the lemon juice and zest, sugar, and water in a pan; boil until the sugar has dissolved.

2. Add the strawberries, lavender, and citric acid and simmer for 20 minutes. Use a potato masher to crush the strawberries as they cook. Remove from the heat and allow the mixture to cool for 30 minutes.

3. Strain the mixture through a sieve, gently pushing on the pulp to squeeze out the last few drops of juice (see page 11).

4. Pour the syrup into sterilized bottles (see page 11), and store in a cool, dark place. Use within 3 months.

Now try this

Try adding a little to a cup of hot chocolate and top with whipped cream. Add a few lavender flowers as a garnish.

Makes APPROXIMATELY 3 CUPS (700ML)

Rhubarb Syrup

One of the earliest arrivals in the kitchen garden, rhubarb is most often stewed or used in baking. However, it makes a delicious syrup, with a beautiful pink hue.

1 pound (450g) rhubarb

1 unwaxed lemon

1 vanilla bean

2 cups, rounded (480g) superfine (caster) sugar

2 cloves

3¾ cups (900ml) water

1 teaspoon citric acid

1. Remove the leaves and trim the bottom edges of the rhubarb; chop roughly. Cut the lemon into quarters. Slit the vanilla bean lengthwise and scrape out the seeds for use in the syrup.

2. Put the rhubarb, lemon, sugar, cloves, vanilla seeds, and water into a pan. Bring to a boil, being careful not to burn the rhubarb.

3. Once the sugar has completely dissolved, add the citric acid and turn the heat down to a gentle simmer. Continue simmering for 20 minutes or until all of the rhubarb is soft. Remove from the heat and allow to cool for 2 hours.

4. Strain the mixture through a sieve (see page 11). If you like your syrup clear, strain again through a piece of fine muslin or cheesecloth.

5. Pour the syrup into sterilized bottles (see page 11) and store in a cool, dark place. It will last there for up to 3 months. Alternatively, you can freeze some of the syrup to make it last longer (see page 11).

Makes APPROXIMATELY 3½ CUPS (900ML)

Rhubarb, Lemon, & Rosemary Syrup

This is a fun syrup to serve to guests. Most can quickly recognize the rhubarb and lemon flavors; but the astonished looks when the mystery ingredient, rosemary, is revealed are quite amusing. You, too, may be amazed at how successful this combination is. Rosemary signifies love, friendship, and trust, so make this for a special person. For a delicious teatime treat, keep the pulp (removing the rosemary stalks), and add to a sponge cake recipe.

2 large sprigs fresh rosemary

1 pound (450g) rhubarb

2 cups, rounded (450g) superfine (caster) sugar

2 unwaxed lemons, juice and zest

4 cups (1 liter) water

1 teaspoon citric acid

1. Rinse the rosemary, and chop the rhubarb into chunks.

2. Put these ingredients in a large pan, along with the sugar, lemon juice and zest, water, and citric acid, and bring to a boil. Remove from the heat and allow to cool for 2 hours.

3. Strain through a sieve lined with muslin (see page 11); give the remaining pulp a good squeeze to extract all of the juice.

4. Pour into sterilized bottles (see page 11). Store in a cool, dark place. Use within 3 months.

Makes APPROXIMATELY 5 CUPS (1.2 LITERS)

Passion Fruit Syrup

Although passion fruit is not native to northern climes, you can find it in larger supermarkets year-round. The unassuming exterior of the fruit hides a scrumptious center with an equally mouthwatering aroma, and this surprisingly easy-to-make syrup has an outstanding finish. Try pouring a little over chocolate ice cream.

16 passion fruits

1 cup (225g) superfine (caster) sugar

1 cup (240ml) fresh lemon juice

1½ cups (360ml) water

1. Cut the passion fruits in half and scrape the pulp into a bowl.

2. Put the sugar, lemon juice, and water into a pan. Bring to a boil, stirring until all the sugar has dissolved.

3. Turn down the heat and add the passion fruit pulp. Stir until well mixed, keeping at a gentle simmer for another 20 minutes.

4. Remove from the heat, cover with a clean dish towel, and let steep overnight.

5. Strain through a fine sieve, pushing gently on the pulp to squeeze out all the juice (see page 11).

6. Pour into sterilized bottles (see page 11) and store in a cool, dark place. Once opened, use within 4 weeks. Alternatively, freeze in small batches for later use (see page 11).

Makes APPROXIMATELY 3 CUPS (700ML)

Mango & Ginger Syrup

This recipe has a tropical note, conjuring up images of white, sandy beaches and an azure sea. It makes a perfect drink for a lazy afternoon in a hammock. Mix the syrup with coconut milk and freeze to make ice pops.

1 large, very ripe mango—approximately 1¼lb (570g)

2-inch (5-cm) piece ginger root

1 vanilla bean

1⅝ cups (375g) superfine (caster) sugar

1 unwaxed lemon

¾ teaspoon citric acid

2 cups (500ml) water

1. Peel the mango and cut the flesh away from the pit. Peel the ginger and crush the flesh with a rolling pin, or use a mortar and pestle. Slice the vanilla bean in half lengthwise and scrape out the seeds; reserve. Cut the lemon into quarters.

2. Put the mango, ginger, vanilla seeds, lemon, sugar, citric acid, and water in a pan. Bring to a boil, stirring until all the sugar is dissolved. Reduce the heat and simmer for another 20 minutes, stirring constantly. Remove from the heat and allow to cool for 30 minutes.

3. Strain the mixture through a fine sieve (see page 11).

4. Pour the syrup into sterilized bottles (see page 11), then store in a cool, dark place. Use within 1 month.

Now try this

Drizzle it over a salad of lettuce, fresh mango, and halloumi cheese.

It will give a sweet and mildly spicy kick to a summer lunch.

Makes APPROXIMATELY 6 CUPS (1.4 LITERS)

Black Currant Syrup

Although very popular in Britain, black currants are not widely known in the United States (though the prohibitions against growing them, for ecological reasons, have now generally been lifted). If you can grow black currants in your state, do plant one of these shrubs. The berries have a rich, complex flavor—sweet, savory, and tart—and they have many health benefits, being especially high in vitamin C.

6 cups (900g) black currants

2 cups, rounded (500g) superfine (caster) sugar

3 cups (700ml) water

1 unwaxed lemon, juice and zest

1 teaspoon citric acid

1. Remove all the stalks from the berries and gently wash the fruit.

2. Put the berries in a large pan, along with the sugar and water, and heat slowly until all the sugar has dissolved. Then turn up the heat and bring the mixture to a gentle simmer; let it simmer for 5 minutes.

3. Add the lemon juice and zest and the citric acid and bring the mixture back to a simmer for another 5 minutes. Remove from the heat and let cool for 10 minutes.

4. Strain through a sieve lined with fine muslin or cheesecloth, pushing the pulp with the back of a spoon to get the last of the juice, while keeping out the pulp as much as possible (see page 11).

5. Pour the syrup into sterilized bottles (see page 11) and store in a cool, dark place. Use within 3 months. Alternatively, pour into plastic bottles to keep in the freezer.

Now try this

Try using this syrup in a marinade for pork or drizzle a little over some ginger ice cream.

Makes APPROXIMATELY 6½ CUPS (1.5 LITERS)

Summer Syrup

It's a wonderful thing, on a hot summer's day, to stand among rows of raspberries, with just the humming of a passing bee for company, eating as many raspberries as you put into your basket. Or blackberries, or cherries... Freeze some of this cordial in an ice cube tray. Then put a few ice cubes in a highball glass and fill it up with fizzy lemonade; the ice cubes will melt, creating a delightful color contrast.

3 cups (400g) cherries

2½ cups, rounded (300g) raspberries

2½ cups, rounded (300g) strawberries

2½ cups (300g) blackberries

2 cups (300g) red currants (or mixed black and red currants)

2 unwaxed lemons

1¾ cups (400g) superfine (caster) sugar

½ teaspoon fennel seeds

2 cardamom pods

5 cups (1.2 liters) water

1½ teaspoons citric acid

1. Rinse the fruit carefully under running water. Remove the stalks from the cherries; there is no need to remove the pits, which will be strained out. Cut the lemons into quarters.

2. Put the fruit in a large pan with the sugar, fennel seed, cardamom pods, and water. Bring the mixture to a boil, stirring to make sure the sugar has dissolved. Turn down the heat, add the citric acid, and allow to simmer for another 20 minutes. Remove from the heat, cover with a clean dish towel, and allow to cool for at least 2 hours.

3. Strain through a fine sieve, pressing firmly on the pulp to make sure all the juice is squeezed out. To clarify further, strain again through a jelly bag or a piece of fine muslin or cheesecloth (see page 11).

4. Pour into sterilized bottles (see page 11); store in a cool, dark place. Use within 3 months. Alternatively, freeze in an ice-cube tray (see page 11).

Makes APPROXIMATELY 7½ CUPS (1.8 LITERS)

Autumn Harvest Syrup

Fall is the most plentiful time of the year when it comes to free fruit; almost everywhere you look there will be a glut of fruit to make use of. Perhaps you have an apple, pear, or plum tree that needs picking—or a neighbor has one. Or you may have a bramble patch full of delicious blackberries at the end of your garden that has not been cleared during the summer. All of these and more can be found close by and will give you a valuable harvest, well worth the effort.

1lb 2oz (500g) apples (6 small)

14oz (400g) plums
(4 medium size)

3 cups (350g) blackberries

1 cup (150g) black currants or
red currants

1 unwaxed lemon

2¼ cups (500g) superfine

(caster) sugar

6½ cups (1.5 liters) water

1 stick cinnamon

6 allspice berries

1 star anise

2 teaspoons citric acid

1. Core and peel the apples. Wash and halve the plums, removing the pits. Rinse the blackberries and the currants in water. Cut the lemon into quarters.

2. Put the sugar, lemon, and spices in a pan, along with the water. Bring to a boil and stir until all of the sugar has dissolved. Reduce the heat. Add the apples, plums, blackberries, currants, and citric acid and simmer for another 20 minutes, or until all the fruit has been reduced to a pulp.

3. Remove from the heat, cover with a clean dish towel, and allow to cool for 2 hours.

4. Strain the mixture through a fine sieve, taking care to squeeze as much juice out of the pulp as possible (see page 11). Then strain again, this time through a jelly bag or piece of fine muslin or cheesecloth.

5. Pour the syrup into sterilized bottles (see page 11) and store it in a cool, dark place. It will usually last into the cold winter months. For added longevity it could be frozen (see page 11).

Makes APPROXIMATELY 10 CUPS (2.4 LITERS)

Mulberry & Cardamom Syrup

Fresh mulberries can be hard to find, but if you're fortunate enough to have a bush growing in your garden, or know of someone who has, do make some of this exotic syrup. Warning: picking mulberries is a really messy job, so go prepared and do not wear white! Try making meringues flavored with cardamom seed and serve them with whipped cream, a few mulberries, a drizzle of the syrup, and, to finish, a few chopped pistachios on top.

5 cups (600g) mulberries

4 cardmom pods

⅞ cup (200g) superfine (caster) sugar

2 cups (500ml) water

1 unwaxed lemon

½ teaspoon citric acid

1. Cut the lemon into quarters.

2. Put the mulberries, cardamom pods, sugar, lemon pieces, and water in a pan. Bring to a boil, stirring continuously until the sugar has dissolved. Reduce the heat and let simmer for another 15 minutes. Mash any whole mulberries with the back of the spoon. Do the same with the cardamom pods once they have softened.

3. Once the mulberries have been reduced to a pulp, remove the pan from the heat and cover with a saucepan lid or dish towel. Let cool for about 2 hours.

4. Strain the mixture through a fine sieve and then through a jelly bag or piece of fine muslin or cheesecloth (see page 11).

5. Pour the syrup into sterilized bottles (see page 11) and store in a cool, dark place. Use within 3 months.

Makes APPROXIMATELY 3½ CUPS (800ML)

Orange, Echinacea, & Lemongrass Syrup

We all know that echinacea is reputed to be effective against coughs and colds. In addition, it has a lovely earthy taste that offsets the sharpness of the oranges in this syrup. Pour some of this syrup sparingly over half a grapefruit for a refreshing taste treat.

1 stem lemongrass

16 oranges: zest of 2, juice of all

2¼ cups (500g) superfine (caster) sugar

1½ teaspoons citric acid

2 cups (450ml) water

½ cup (40g) shredded echinacea root

1. Rinse the lemongrass in water and crush it with a rolling pin.

2. Put it in a large pan along with the orange juice and zest, sugar, citric acid, and water. Bring to a boil, stirring until all the sugar has dissolved. Reduce the heat and add the echinacea. Simmer, stirring, for another 5 minutes. Remove from the heat and allow to cool for 1 hour.

3. Strain the mixture through a fine sieve, pushing gently with the spoon to extract all of the juice, then strain again through a jelly bag or a piece of fine muslin or cheesecloth (see page 11).

4. Pour the syrup into sterilized bottles (see page 11) and store in a cool, dark place. Use within 3 months.

Makes APPROXIMATELY 7½ CUPS (1.8 LITERS)

Raspberry & Angelica Syrup

If you haven't got fresh raspberries, you can use frozen ones for this syrup, as raspberries have the ability to hold on to their luscious flavor even after they have been in a freezer. The angelica gives a slight hint of celery to this syrup— a subtle, earthy taste that, however, doesn't detract from the tang of the raspberries.

3½ cups (400g) raspberries

a small bunch of angelica leaves (about 4–5)

1¼ cups, rounded (300g) superfine (caster) sugar

1 unwaxed lemon, juice and zest

1¾ cups (400ml) water

¾ teaspoon citric acid

1. Rinse the angelica leaves under running water. Put them in a pan along with the raspberries, sugar, lemon juice and zest, water, and citric acid. Bring to a boil, stirring constantly until all the sugar has dissolved. Reduce the heat and simmer for another 15 minutes, stirring occasionally. Mash any whole raspberries with the back of the spoon.

2. Remove from the heat, cover with a saucepan lid or dish towel, and let cool for about 2 hours.

3. Strain the syrup through a fine sieve (see page 11) and then through a jelly bag or a piece of fine muslin or cheesecloth.

4. Pour the syrup into sterilized bottles (see page 11) and store it in a cool, dry place; use within 3 months.

Makes APPROXIMATELY 2½ CUPS (600ML)

Raspberry & Lovage Syrup

The fragrantly sweet, yet slightly tart flavor of raspberries is beguiling; there never seems to be enough of them. If you can bear to put some aside for this syrup, you won't be disappointed. Show off its glorious color in a beautiful glass bottle. For a delectable dessert, combine some crushed meringues and sliced peaches and top them with whipped cream mixed with this syrup.

3½ cups (400g) raspberries

a handful of fresh lovage leaves (about 10–15)

1⅓ cups (300g) superfine (caster) sugar

1 lemon, juice and zest

1¾ cups (400ml) water

¾ teaspoon citric acid

1. Rinse the lovage leaves under running water. Put the raspberries, lovage, sugar, lemon juice and zest, and water in a pan. Bring to a boil, stirring continuously until all the sugar has dissolved. Reduce the heat, add the citric acid, and let simmer for another 15 minutes, stirring occasionally and mashing any whole raspberries with the back of the spoon.

2. When the raspberries have been reduced to a pulp, remove from the heat and cover with a saucepan lid or dish towel. Allow to cool for about 2 hours.

3. Strain the mixture through a fine sieve and then through a jelly bag or piece of fine muslin or cheesecloth (see page 11).

4. Pour the syrup into sterilized bottles (see page 11). Store in a cool, dark place; use within 3 months.

Makes APPROXIMATELY 2½ CUPS (600ML)

Raspberry & Rose Syrup

The aroma and flavor of the rose petals really shine through in this syrup, softening the tart edge of the strong-flavored fruit, without imposing an overtly floral taste on it. Dilute the syrup to taste with sparkling or soda water.

2 large sprigs fresh rosemary

1lb (450g) rhubarb

2 cups, rounded (450g) superfine (caster) sugar

2 unwaxed lemons, juice and zest

4 cups (1 liter) water

1 teaspoon citric acid

1. Put the raspberries, sugar, lemon juice and zest, citric acid, and water in a saucepan. Bring to a boil, then simmer for 15 minutes.

2. Remove from the heat and let cool for 30 minutes.

3. Put the rose petals in a large bowl and pour the syrup over them. Cover with a clean dish towel and let steep overnight.

4. Strain the syrup through a piece of fine muslin or cheesecloth (see page 11).

5. Pour the syrup into sterilized bottles (see page 11). It will keep in a cool, dark place for up to 3 months.

Now try this

Mix the syrup with water and gelatin, following the instructions on the packet. When the mixture starts to set, add in a few extra rose petals so they are suspended in it. (A glass bowl will display the effect beautifully.) Serve with vanilla ice cream.

Makes APPROXIMATELY 4 CUPS (1 LITER)

Raspberry & Orange Syrup

Combining these two strong-flavored fruits creates a real taste sensation. This is a good way to use up a surplus of raspberries to prevent them from going off. Children can enjoy using it to make their own ice pops and lollies. Dilute the juice to taste with sparkling water. Or add a drop or two to a glass of fizzy lemonade.

6 cups (700g) raspberries

1⅓ cups (300g) superfine (caster) sugar

2 cups (500ml) water

6 oranges, zest and juice

1 teaspoon citric acid

1. Put the raspberries, sugar, and water in a saucepan. Bring to the boil and cook until all the raspberries have been reduced to a pulp. Reduce the heat and add the orange juice and zest and citric acid. Bring back to a boil.

2. Allow the syrup to cool for around 30–45 minutes then strain it through a piece of fine muslin or cheesecloth (see page 11).

3. Pour the syrup into sterilized bottles (see page 11). It will keep for up to 3 months when stored in a cool, dark place.

Makes APPROXIMATELY 4 CUPS (1 LITER)

Lemon Verbena & Raspberry Syrup

Lemon verbena (*Aloysia citrodora*) is a little-known but absolutely delicious herb. It's nothing to look at—although the tiny, lavender-white flowers on this tall, leggy shrub are quite cute—but the smell and taste of those little leaves pack such a lemony, aromatic, sweet punch. It's a natural bedfellow for raspberries and you really don't need many leaves to get fantastic results.

2 cups (500ml) water

2 cups (400g) superfine (caster) sugar

1 cup (125g) raspberries

4 lemon verbena leaves

1. Stir the water and sugar together in a nonreactive pan over a low heat to make a simple syrup. Once it has reached boiling point, add the raspberries and lemon verbena leaves, stir, and let simmer until the raspberries have collapsed (about 10 minutes).

2. Strain while still piping hot, but not boiling, into a wide-mouthed pitcher—you really don't want raspberry pips in this syrup—then funnel into the sterilized bottle(s) (see page 11). Seal and store in the refrigerator for up to 2 weeks. The remaining raspberry (with the lemon verbena solids removed) can be used as a compote over yogurt or ice cream.

Makes APPROXIMATELY 2 CUPS (500ML)

Honeysuckle Syrup

A hedgerow or wall covered in wild honeysuckle (*Lonicera periclymenum*) is a heady feast for the senses. *Lonicera japonica* is equally sweet and delicious and, like wild honeysuckle, can be found naturalized across Europe and North America, scrambling over gardens, walls, and wasteland. Honeysuckle has the strongest scent at night, so try to harvest unopened and newly opened flowers during the evening (how's that for a romantic date suggestion?) or early morning.

8 large handfuls of unsprayed honeysuckle flowers, leaves and stems removed

2 cups (400g) superfine (caster) sugar

juice of ½ lemon

1. Place the honeysuckle flowers in a nonreactive bowl and cover with cold water, then leave to steep for 12 hours, or at least overnight, at room temperature. Make sure the flowers are completely covered by the water.

2. Strain the mixture into a measuring cup, discarding the flowers. Pour the liquid into a nonreactive pan. Measure an equal amount of sugar to the liquid and add to the pan. Bring to a boil, and let simmer for 5 minutes. Feel free to replace half the sugar with a handful of chopped sweet cicely leaves, but bear in mind that this will adjust the color.

3. Remove from the heat, let cool, add the lemon juice, and funnel into the sterilized presentation bottle(s) (see page 11).

Makes APPROXIMATELY 2 CUPS (500ML)

Chocolate Mint Syrup

The menthol in peppermint often makes it too sharp for drinks, but there is an exception: chocolate mint (*Mentha piperita f. citrata* 'Chocolate'). Try combining it with spearmint (*Mentha spicata*), also known as garden, or common, mint, in this recipe, which gives the gorgeous chocolate undertones of after-dinner mints but not too much peppermint. If you don't have chocolate mint, just double up on whichever mint you do have.

1 cup (250ml) water

1 cup (200g) superfine (caster) sugar

½ cup (about 15) unsprayed spearmint leaves, stalks removed

1. Stir the water and sugar together in a nonreactive pan over a low heat and let simmer for 2 minutes. Smack the unwashed mint leaves between your palms to release the oils and drop them into the pan. Immediately remove the pan from the heat. Let the leaves infuse for 10 minutes—no longer or you will lose some of the freshness of the mint and it will start to take on bitterness.

2. While still piping hot, strain the liquid into a wide-mouthed pitcher, then funnel into a sterilized bottle (see page 11) and seal. Store in the refrigerator for up to 2 weeks.

Makes APPROXIMATELY 1 CUP (250ML)

Fig, Peach, & Vanilla Syrup

This combination creates a deliciously smooth flavor—the vanilla taking the sharp edge off the peaches and the figs lending their own subtle, mellow taste. Hide this one, as you won't want to share it! Try pouring a little of this syrup over peaches or figs baked in puff pastry, dusted with confectioners' (icing) sugar.

14lb (400g) figs (14–16)

¾lb (340g) peaches (3 small)

½ vanilla bean

1 unwaxed lemon, juice and zest

⅓ cup (80g) superfine (caster) sugar

3½ cups (820ml) water

¾ teaspoon citric acid

1. Trim the stalks from the figs. Peel the peaches, remove the pits, and cut into quarters. Scrape the seeds from the vanilla bean half and reserve.

2. Put the lemon juice and zest, sugar, and water in a pan and bring to a boil, stirring until all the sugar has dissolved. Reduce the heat and add the figs, peaches, vanilla seeds, and citric acid. Simmer until the fruit is soft, about 15 minutes.

3. Remove from the heat and let cool for 30 minutes.

4. Strain the mixture through a fine sieve (see page 11).

5. Pour the syrup into sterilized bottles (see page 11) and store in a cool, dark place. Use within 3 months.

Makes APPROXIMATELY 3¼ CUPS (800ML)

Homemade Cola Cordial

Okay, you may argue that nothing quite beats the "real thing", but there's something quite rewarding about "cracking" the recipe and sipping smugly on your own homemade version.

1 cup (200g) granulated sugar

1 cup (200g) dark muscovado sugar

2 cups (500ml) water

1 vanilla bean/pod, seeded

1 cinnamon stick

a pinch of nutmeg

pared zest of 1 orange

pared zest of 1 lemon

pared zest of 1 lime

1. Put the granulated and muscovado sugar and 2 cups (500ml) of water in a large saucepan set over medium heat. Simmer gently, stirring frequently, until the sugar has dissolved.

2. Turn down the heat and add the vanilla bean/pod, cinnamon, nutmeg, and the zests of the citrus fruit. Allow to simmer for 2 hours over a low heat, stirring occasionally, until it has reduced to a thin syrup.

3. Leave the cordial to cool and then pass though a strainer and pour into a sterilized bottle (see page 11). It will keep for one month in the fridge.

Makes APPROXIMATELY 2 CUPS (500ML)

Chapter 5

Lemonades

Classic Lemonade

Although a little time-consuming initially, compared to the
simplest form of fresh lemonade, this recipe for a lemon syrup
will enable you to conjure up a pitcher of refreshing lemonade
at short notice on a hot summer's day. And if your children
normally swig fizzy lemonade, they may enjoy discovering this
natural alternative. Dilute the lemonade to taste with still,
sparkling, or soda water. You can also use it, diluted 1 part
lemonade to 2 parts water, to make ice pops.

zest of 1 unwaxed lemon

1¾ cups (400g) superfine
(caster) sugar

2⅓ cups (550ml) water

2⅓ cups (550ml) lemon juice
(about 12 lemons)

1. Put the lemon zest, sugar, and water in a pan. Bring to a boil.
   Simmer, stirring, until all the sugar has dissolved.

2. Add the lemon juice, including some of the flesh if you prefer
   the lemonade to have a little texture, and bring the mixture back
   to a boil, stirring constantly.

3. Remove from the heat and allow to cool for 1 hour.

4. Pour the liquid into sterilized bottles (see page 11). It will keep
   in a cool, dark place or in the fridge for up to 2 months.

Makes APPROXIMATELY 5 CUPS (1.2 LITERS)

Rose Lemonade

This lemonade has a lovely perfume, and if you like floral drinks it will become a favorite.

zest of 1 unwaxed lemon

1¾ cups (400g) superfine (caster) sugar

2⅓ cups (550ml) water

2⅓ cups (550ml) lemon juice (about 12 lemons)

4½ cups (50g) rose petals (see Note)

1. Put the lemon zest, sugar, and water in a pan and bring to a boil. Simmer, stirring, until all the sugar has dissolved.

2. Add the lemon juice, including some of the flesh if you prefer the lemonade to have a little texture, and bring the mixture back to a boil, stirring constantly.

3. Remove from the heat and allow to cool for 1 hour.

4. Put the rose petals in a large bowl. Pour the liquid over the petals, cover the bowl with a clean dish cloth, and let steep overnight.

5. Strain the liquid through a fine sieve (see page 11) and pour into sterilized bottles (see page 11). It will keep in a cool, dark place or in the fridge for up to 2 months.

Note

If you are using fresh rose petals, make sure they have not been sprayed with any chemicals; if in any doubt, buy dried rose petals from a good herbalist.

Makes APPROXIMATELY 5 CUPS (1.2 LITERS)

Lavender Lemonade

Edible plants are growing in popularity, brightening up plates in lots of brilliant restuarants, and chefs are always looking for new and interesting ways to use them in cooking. Here, garnish your diluted lemonade with a couple of heads of lavender. Or freeze some of the flowers into ice cubes—this looks stunning.

2 large sprigs fresh rosemary

1 pound (450g) rhubarb

2 cups, rounded (450g) superfine (caster) sugar

2 unwaxed lemons, juice and zest

4 cups (1 liter) water

1 teaspoon citric acid

1. Put the lemon zest, sugar, and water in a pan and bring to a boil. Simmer, stirring, until all the sugar has dissolved.

2. Add the lemon juice, including some of the flesh if you prefer the lemonade to have a little texture, and bring the mixture back to a boil, stirring constantly.

3. Remove from the heat and add the lavender heads. Allow to cool for 1 hour.

4. Strain the mixture (see page 11), then pour it into sterilized bottles (see page 11). It will keep in a cool, dark place or in the fridge for up to 2 months.

Makes APPROXIMATELY 5 CUPS (1.2 LITERS)

Lavender & Ginger Lemonade

This is a truly delightful mix of flavors that work really well together. Give it a try—this may become the favorite of the summer. But you can also enjoy it in the depths of winter, when we are craving the start of spring and the delights of summer. Simply place the lavender heads in a jar along with the sugar and leave the jar in a cool, dark place until needed. Ginger, of course, is available throughout the year.

2-inch (5-cm) piece of fresh ginger root

1¾ cups (400g) superfine (caster) sugar

zest of 1 unwaxed lemon

2⅓ cups (550ml) water

2⅓ cups (550ml) lemon juice (about 12 lemons)

15 heads of lavender (see page 13)

1. Peel the ginger and crush it with a rolling pin. Put it in a pan with the sugar, lemon zest, and water. Bring to a boil. Simmer, stirring, to make sure all the sugar has dissolved.

2. Add the lemon juice, including some of the flesh if you prefer the lemonade to have a little texture, and bring the mixture back to a boil, stirring constantly.

3. Remove from the heat and allow to cool for 1 hour.

4. Place the lavender in one or more sterilized bottles (see page 11). Remove the pieces of ginger from the pan and discard.

5. Pour the liquid into the bottle(s). It will keep in a cool, dark place or in the fridge for up to 2 months.

Makes APPROXIMATELY 5 CUPS (1.2 LITERS)

Pink Lemonade

Cranberries give this lemonade a lovely color as well as extra flavor and pizzazz. This is great for taking on a picnic or serving at a special summer afternoon party. So plan ahead: freeze some cranberries in December for use in summer. Dilute to taste with your choice of water. You might also make it into a granita: put the diluted lemonade into an ice cream maker until it is slushy.

2 cups (200g) cranberries

2¼ cups (500g) superfine (caster) sugar

zest of 1 unwaxed lemon

2⅓ cups (550ml) water

2⅓ cups (550ml) lemon juice (about 12 lemons)

1. Put the cranberries, sugar, lemon zest, and water in a pan. Bring to a boil. Simmer, stirring, until all the sugar has dissolved and all the cranberries have split. Give them some help with a potato masher, if necessary.

2. Add the lemon juice, including some of the flesh if you prefer the lemonade to have a little texture, and bring the mixture back to a boil, stirring constantly.

3. Remove from the heat and allow to cool for 1 hour.

4. Strain the liquid through a fine sieve (see page 11). Add the lemon flesh, if desired, at this point.

5. Pour the liquid into sterilized bottles. It will keep in a cool, dark place or in the fridge for up to 2 months.

Makes APPROXIMATELY 5 CUPS (1.2 LITERS)

Geranium Lemonade

This ingenious recipe always gets a surprised reaction from guests, as many people do not realize that scented geraniums can be used for culinary purposes. Try some of the different varieties, such as "Orange Fizz" and "Concolor Lace."

zest of 1 unwaxed lemon

2½ cups (550g) superfine (caster) sugar

2⅓ cups (550ml) water

2⅓ cups (550ml) lemon juice (about 12 lemons)

10 scented geranium leaves in good condition

1. Put the lemon zest, sugar, and water in a pan and bring to a boil. Simmer, stirring, until all the sugar has dissolved.

2. Add the lemon juice, including some of the flesh if you prefer the lemonade to have a little texture, and bring the mixture back to a boil, stirring constantly.

3. Remove from the heat and allow to cool for 1 hour.

4. Place the geranium leaves in a bowl. Pour the liquid over them, cover with a clean dish towel, and let steep overnight.

5. Remove the leaves and pour the liquid into sterilized bottles (see page 11). It will keep in a cool, dark place or in the fridge for up to 2 months.

Now try this

As an alternative to serving this as a drink, use it to flavor a sponge cake. Place a few geranium leaves in the bottom of the greased cake pan, then pour the cake batter on top. When the cake has been baked and cooled, remove the leaves from the bottom, turn the cake right side up, and ice it with a mixture of confectioners' (icing) sugar and the undiluted geranium lemonade.

Makes APPROXIMATELY 5 CUPS (1.2 LITERS)

Limeade

There is no harm in cheating a little every now and then, so save yourself a lot of time and expense by using purchased, bottled, unsweetened lime juice—available in supermarkets—for most of the juice required for this recipe. Adding the flesh of the three fresh limes required will give this lovely, refreshing drink some depth. Garnish each glass of diluted limeade with a slice of lime.

zest of 3 limes

1¾ cups (400g) superfine (caster) sugar

1 teaspoon citric acid

2⅓ cups (550ml) water

2⅓ cups (550ml) lime juice (20–25 limes, or 3 limes used for zest plus purchased lime juice to fill)

1. Put the lime zest, sugar, citric acid, and water in a pan and bring to a boil. Simmer, stirring, until all the sugar has dissolved.

2. Add the lime juice, including some of the flesh if you prefer the limeade to have a little texture, and bring back to a boil, stirring constantly.

3. Remove from the heat and allow to cool for 1 hour.

4. Pour the liquid into sterilized bottles (see page 11). It will keep in a cool, dark place or in the fridge for up to 2 months.

Makes APPROXIMATELY 5 CUPS (1.2 LITERS)

Elderflower Lemonade

Elderflower is such a versatile ingredient, one that works in many different drink recipes; it gives a beautiful flowery edge—though a very subtle one in this lemonade. If you want to use these wonderful flowers in a recipe, you'll need to be quick, as their season is fleeting.

zest of 1 unwaxed lemon

1¾ cups (400g) superfine (caster) sugar

2⅓ cups (550ml) water

2⅓ cups (550ml) lemon juice (about 12 lemons)

6 heads of elderflower (see page 13)

1. Put the lemon zest, sugar, and water in a pan and bring to a boil. Simmer, stirring, until all the sugar has dissolved.

2. Add the lemon juice and bring the mixture back to a boil, stirring constantly.

3. Remove from the heat and allow to cool for 1 hour.

4. Put the elderflowers in a large bowl. Pour the liquid over the flowers, cover with a clean dish towel, and let steep overnight.

5. Strain the liquid through a fine sieve (see page 11) and pour into sterilized bottles (see page 11). It will keep in a cool, dark place or in the fridge for up to 2 months.

Makes APPROXIMATELY 5 CUPS (1.2 LITERS)

Orangeade

Blood oranges taste great when made into a syrup and they have the most wonderful color; but don't worry if you can't find these—ordinary oranges will work just as well. This drink is fun and simple to prepare and is great for brunch or an afternoon party.

zest of 2 oranges

1¾ cups (400g) superfine (caster) sugar

1 teaspoon citric acid

2⅓ cups (550ml) water

2⅓ cups (550ml) freshly squeezed orange juice (about 12 oranges)

1. Put the orange zest, sugar, citric acid, and water in a pan and bring to a boil. Simmer, stirring, until all the sugar has dissolved.

2. Add the orange juice, including some of the flesh if you prefer the orangeade to have a little texture, and bring the mixture back to a boil, stirring constantly.

3. Remove from the heat and allow to cool for 1 hour.

4. Pour the liquid into sterilized bottles (see page 11). It will keep in a cool, dark place or in the fridge for up to 2 months.

Makes APPROXIMATELY 5 CUPS (1.2 LITERS)

Apple Lemonade

This recipe is best made with cooking apples—they turn to delicious apple-flavored foam when boiled. Cooked apple drinks are usually pale, but fresh juices made from red apples will be pink if you juice them with the skins on. For a much quicker result, use fresh apple juice, omit the sugar, add the fresh lemon juice and fill with sparkling mineral water.

2–3 cooking apples, unpeeled, chopped into small pieces

sugar, to taste

freshly squeezed juice of 1 lemon

sparkling mineral water, to top up

ice cubes, to serve

1. Put the apples in a saucepan, cover with cold water, bring to the boil and simmer until soft.

2. Strain, pressing the pulp through fine sieve with a spoon (see page 11). Add sugar to taste, stir until dissolved, then leave to cool.

3. To serve, pack a pitcher (jug) with ice, half-fill a glass with the apple juice, add the lemon juice, and top up with the sparkling water.

Makes APPROXIMATELY 2 CUPS (500ML)

Red Clover Lemonade

The beautiful flowers of red clover (*Trifolium pratense*) are slightly sweet, and many of us will have enjoyed them in clover honey. They are also packed with nutrients, calcium, magnesium, potassium, and vitamin C. Red clover has been used in tea form for many years to alleviate the symptoms of gout. This lemonade is a quick and easy recipe that leaves you with a very pretty, delicately flavored sweet drink—think sweet hay.

3 cups (750ml) water

Approximately 40 red clover blossoms

1 cup (250ml) freshly squeezed lemon juice

3 tbsp (50ml) honey, preferably raw, set or runny

1. Bring the water to a slow boil in the nonreactive pan, add the clover blossoms, and simmer gently for 5 minutes.

2. Strain the liquid into a wide-mouthed pitcher (jug), removing the blossoms, and return to the cleaned pan over a low heat. Add the lemon juice and honey, and stir to dissolve the honey. Do not let it boil.

3. Remove from the heat and allow to cool. Pour the lemonade into sterilized bottles (see page 11) and store in the refrigerator until ready to serve—it will keep for 1 month.

Makes APPROXIMATELY 4 CUPS (1 LITER)

Strawberry & Mint Lemonade

It's a mystery why people prefer to buy lemonade when it's so easy to make at home. Freshly made lemonade combined with fresh blended strawberries and decorated with a mint sprig is as pleasant an assault on the nostrils as one can imagine.

20 ripe strawberries

⅔ cup (160ml) fresh lemon juice (about 4 lemons)

grated zest of 4 lemons

6 tablespoons superfine (caster) sugar

1 large handful of fresh mint

soda water, to top up

mint sprigs, to garnish

ice cubes, to serve

1. Put the strawberries in a blender and blitz to a purée.

2. Add the lemon juice and zest, sugar, and mint to a large pitcher (jug) and stir until the sugar has dissolved. Fill the pitcher with ice, add the blended strawberries, and top up with soda water.

3. Serve in ice-filled highball glasses, garnished with a mint sprig.

Makes APPROXIMATELY 2 CUPS (500ML)

Rhubarb Strawberryade

This unusual, old-fashioned drink is based on homemade lemonade. Make it with pretty pink forced rhubarb for an utterly stunning color, or add a dash of grenadine to point up the pink.

1lb 2oz (500g) rhubarb, trimmed and sliced

2 tablespoons icing (confectioners') sugar

1 unwaxed lemon, juice and zest

4 cups (1 liter) boiling water, or to cover

6 strawberries, hulled and halved

1. Put the rhubarb, sugar, and lemon zest into a saucepan and cover with the boiling water. Stew until the rhubarb is very soft.

2. Add the strawberries and boil hard for about 1 minute, then strain into sterilized bottles (see page 11), cool, and keep in the refrigerator.

Makes APPROXIMATELY 2 CUPS (500ML)

Honey Grape Lemonade

On a hot summer day, this quick, easy, and refreshing old-fashioned crowd pleaser made with just a few ingredients is all you need to chill out, and the kids will thank you!

4 cups (1 liter) white grape juice

juice of 5 large lemons

2½ cups (600ml) water

honey, to taste

12 small ice cubes

2 lemons, thinly sliced

ice cubes, to serve

1. In a large pitcher (jug), mix together the grape juice, lemon juice, and water. Stir well.

2. Add honey to sweeten, to taste. Add ice cubes. Chill for 1 hour before serving. Float with lemon slices.

Makes APPROXIMATELY 7½ CUPS (1.8 LITERS)

Index

Recipe Credits

Maxine Clark
48

Lyndel Costain & Nicola Grimes
21, 25, 28

Tonia George
32, 47

Beshlie Grimes
68, 69, 70, 74, 75, 76, 77, 78, 79, 80, 82, 83, 84,
86, 87, 88, 89, 90, 91, 92, 93, 94, 97, 98, 99,
100, 105, 110, 112, 113, 114, 115, 116, 117. 118,
119

Carol Hilker
64

Lottie Muir
60, 72, 73, 101, 102, 104, 122

Fifi O'Neill
61, 126

Elsa Petersen-Schepelern
23, 30, 34, 35, 44, 45, 46, 120, 124

Louise Pickford
20, 22, 33, 36, 38, 39, 40, 41, 58, 62, 65

Ben Reed
24, 26, 27, 29, 42, 52, 54, 55, 56, 57, 107, 123